This is a great book about rea[...] put it down! It is well written and is a must for every m[...] and daughter.

—Edith Stauffer
President and Director of Psychosynthesis International
Author of *Unconditional Love and Forgiveness*

This is a terrific book: warm, intimate, and full of love. It is the product of a mature, compassionate woman who has emerged from the grief and loss resulting from giving up a child, to discover a place of openness, security and joy. It is the story of two remarkable women who, because of their love for one child, create a deep friendship together. Their bond invites their shared child into a womb of love and acceptance, and weaves a healing web of connection for both families.

Louise Jurgens' courage, vulnerability and trust shine through every page. Her inner journey of courage and self-transformation mirrors her epic search for her child. Among all the books on adoption published, this one shines like a radiant gem.

—Suzanne Arms
Author of *Adoption: A Handful of Hope*

I wish I could have read *Torn from the Heart* before I began my search for my birthson, Mykel. I would have been better prepared for the emotional but worthwhile roller coaster ride I was about to embark on.

—Linda Maupin
Birthmother

Torn from the Heart tells the moving story of one birthmother's search for the daughter she surrendered to adoption. It is a valuable addition to the adoption literature because it presents an example of the struggles of young mothers to heal from the profound loss of babies lost to them through adoption, and because it records the courage and persistence of one such mother to find and meet her child.

The book also provides a sensitive picture of the dilemma of the adoptive mother who wants what is best for her child but is unsure about the value or impact of a reunion, and of an adopted daughter opening herself to feelings long denied. As important is Ms. Jurgens' honest account of the ongoing struggle that she and daughter have had in making an intimate connection. Her book makes clear that reunion does not end the lifelong pain of a loss through adoption; rather it provides a significant opportunity for healing old wounds and the challenge of a new relationship. Members of the adoption triangle, adoption workers, and clinicians involved with triangle members would all do well to read *Torn from the Heart*.

—Kenneth W. Watson
Board of Directors, American Adoption Congress
Co-author, *Adoption and the Family*

Unforgettable! Stunning in its courage and wrenching in its honesty, *Torn from the Heart* is the story of young Rosanne and her two mothers—Louise, who gave birth to her and never forgot her or gave up searching for her, and Rose, who adopted Rosanne as an infant and cherished her into adulthood . . . a poignantly-moving testament to two women whose capacity for love enabled them to form a caring bond with one another for the sake of the daughter they share.

—Michelle Morris
Adoptive mother; author of *If I Should Die Before I Wake*

Words cannot begin to express my emotions, feelings and love to a most courageous lady. I had no idea the impact this book would have on my life. It has given me the hope of finding out about my own heritage.

—Marilyn Cook
Adult adoptee

A deeply touching account of a birthmother's emotional experience and healing process regarding the daughter she had, gave up for adoption, and then, with courage, found.

—Sherry Larkin, LCSW
Birthmother

Jurgens tells her story dispassionately, allowing the drama to speak for itself. She refrains from holding the adoption system responsible for all her problems. Jurgens makes an important contribution to the search and reunion literature by continuing her story after finding her daughter. She chronicles the development of their relationship, from one that begins tentatively, to a more mature one.

It is hoped that books like Jurgens' will not only change the image of the birthmother, but will also change the image of adoptive parents.

—Lois Melina
Editor and publisher, *Adopted Child*

A heartfelt and poignant account of one of life's most important experiences.

—Annette Baran, MSW, LCSW
Co-author of *The Adoption Triangle*

Inspirational in its courage! This book touched me in such a heartfelt way that I cried most of the way through it. A must reading for everyone concerned with the journey into self-forgiveness and love.

—Elaine Higgins
Adult adoptee

Louise Jurgens has written a personal, courageous account that takes the reader on a powerful, moving journey involving the painful relinquishment of her infant daughter for adoption, a heart-wrenching search, and a re-union that transcends the fears and lack of trust that prevent people from arriving at the truth. *Torn from the Heart* stirs the heart. It is unforgettable. It should be must reading for the millions of people whose lives are touched by adoption as well as those who live outside of the adoption triangle.

—Reuben Pannor
Co-author of *The Adoption Triangle*

Explosive love that knows no bounds! This is a story of love beyond self that extends and recreates its lovely gift. It is a heartwarming inspiration; truly a healing force.

—Roberta K. Tager, MS
Counselor, minister, and holistic healer

TORN FROM THE HEART

The Amazing True Story of a Birthmother's Search for Her Lost Daughter

by Louise Jurgens

Aslan
PUBLISHING

Published by
Aslan Publishing
P.O. Box 108
Lower Lake, CA 95457
(707) 995-1861

For a free catalog of all our titles,
or to order more copies of this book
please call (800) 275-2606

You may contact the author by writing to her at:
P.O. Box 728, Woodbridge, CA 95258-0728

Library of Congress Cataloging-in-Publication Data:

Jurgens, Louise, 1942-
    Torn from the heart : the amazing story of a birthmother's search for
her lost daughter / by Louise Jurgens.
        p. cm.
    ISBN 0-944031-44-7 : $12.95
    1.   Jurgens, Louise, 1942- . 2. Birthmothers—United
States—Biography. 3. Adoption—United States—Psychological aspects.
I. Title. II. Title: Birthmother's search.
    HV874.82.J87A3 1992
    362.82'98--dc20
    [B]
                                                        92-27644
                                                        CIP

Copyright © 1992, Louise Jurgens

Cover concept by Kathleen Vande Kieft
Art direction by Brenda Plowman

Printed in USA
First Edition

10 9 8 7 6 5 4 3 2 1

Table of Contents

This book is dedicated to
Rose White,
a remarkable woman—
my daughter's mother.

Acknowledgments

Many thanks to Michelle Morris, Glenda Hesseltine, Pauline Hale and Judy Withers for their emotional encouragement, wisdom and limitless love.

I am grateful to Becky Magnuson for her typing skill and patience and for learning to guide the manuscript through the computer with the help of Jim Magnuson. Thanks also to Dorothy Maas for her valuable feedback and to Deborah Song for her editing suggestions and love.

My family's contributions were of a different nature. They unknowingly always gave me what I needed to grow. My brother Pete and his wife Donas helped me with their love and enthusiasm as did my brother Al who died before he knew how much his open heart and overflowing love impacted me.

In addition, there are many friends I want to thank for supporting me in a variety of significant ways: Albert and Marlene Abdulky, Vic Ardelean, Inge Asman, Sam Beasly, L. Deano Bertalino, Marilyn and John Cook, Mike Dempewolf, Sara Garfield, Elaine Higgins, Sheri Jennum, Sherry Larkin, Harry Leeper, Rae Mansu, Linda Maupin, Sandy McCullough, Monty Merril, Frank Miyashiro, Dory Nicolas, Sheryl Raumann, Kathryn Reynolds, Teri Roberts, Sara Saric, Shelly Stagno, Roberta Tager, Janice Travis and Bob Valine.

I want also to thank the staff of Aslan Publishing: Dawson Church's editorial assistance was unparalleled and Brenda Plowman and Eileen Duhné's warmth and enthusiasm unequalled. I am blessed that all three are living examples of spiritual light.

Lastly, it is with humble gratitude that I thank Richard Bach, John Bradshaw and Edith Stauffer for writing books during my lifetime which have been catalysts for my personal growth.

This book is autobiographical although some facts and names have been changed in order to protect the privacy of a few individuals.

—*Louise Jurgens,*
Lodi, California

When I look back on this will I be glad I dared,
or glad I didn't?
—RICHARD BACH

No matter what happens, no matter what appears to be,
the only reality is love.
—RICHARD BACH

Preface

Four years ago doctors diagnosed the numbness in my hands as carpal tunnel syndrome. At that time I had seriously begun writing this book, although I had long before conceived its content. However, as I dredged up the nerve to publicly step out of a dark closet of secrecy, I unexpectedly unlocked the door that led me to the frightened child buried deep inside me. Armed with determination, I struggled to give birth to my story, but as it took form my physical symptoms worsened to the extent that the numbness spread to both arms and my left leg. This time the traditional medical establishment diagnosed incurable nerve demyelination and partial muscle atrophy. Fortunately, with each step I took in unraveling my story, the lost child within me began a slow metamorphosis, and gradually, with each unblocked feeling, the liberation of my body began to unfold as well.

What created this physical and emotional trauma? It is my belief that I learned to submerge all genuine feelings to such an extent that what began as emotional numbness became physical as well. On the surface my youth seemed normal enough, but as I looked back and my repressed child began to surface, I realized that I had begun anesthetizing myself from feelings by turning inward in silent shyness years before I began attending school.

How could such a well-meaning girl as I fall into this somber maze? Why would I wait until I was physically ailing and near fifty before allowing myself to unlock and trust my inner feelings? That search led me into the shadowy halls of my past, where I learned far more than I had anticipated.

When I was young, I envisioned being a wife and a mother. I imagined raising and loving a child. Then on August 7, 1961, I gave birth to a baby girl. I was not then anyone's wife, and I had not even the faintest hope of raising my child. Never did I dream I would begin a unique sharing of my daughter with another woman some twenty years later. I was nineteen and could not remotely envision how the events surrounding that birth would alter my life in so many ways.

I am not a famous person. In fact, I love privacy and anonymity. No one knows me beyond relatives, close friends and the students in my classroom. It is my friends who pushed and emotionally supported me to share my story, although I resisted for years. Being a practical person, I grappled with the doubt that this book might never be published. A fear of reopening details of my past which were painful and sad filled me with misgivings.

Ultimately, my reluctance was firmly dispelled when I undeniably understood that the incidents of my life, which are encapsulated in this tale, beg to be told, as they represent a miracle that catapulted me out of hiding and into acceptance and understanding of my childhood legacy. I also felt my story might serve millions of others caught in similar emotional challenges and help those who fear entering this realm of outmoded societal mores.

So I am writing this account. My story necessitates a short trip into the past as most autobiographies do, with the most intense looks directed at that part of my life that society and my parents predicted would stigmatize me were I ever to venture there. Though the ghosts of my childhood perplexed me, I didn't know until my book was near completion that I had entered a murky depth far beyond anything I had imagined.

On one level, the destruction began not in looking at but in the hiding of my secret. When I gave birth, I saw my daughter briefly for five days and was given no option but adoption. The agents of society who took my child said they were protecting me—they were helping me to keep my secret. I played by their rules, as I was unaware of any others. There was an unspoken agreement that I would forget my daughter, and I would thank society and my parents for rescuing me from my mistake. But on a cellular level, I could not repress my pain. No rationalization could mask my guilt, and within weeks of her surrender, I felt that a part of me had been taken away.

I began looking at every baby I saw, feeling there was no end to my regret. My mind was on a runaway journey with no seeming end. Where was my daughter? Was she healthy? Was she in a loving home? There were times when my anguish would surface in tears, but I felt bound and tied to an oath of silence. More often than not, I was so emotionally guarded that I never knew what I was feeling.

Fifteen years later my pain was partially soothed and the illusion that I was unique thoroughly shattered when I read *The Adoption Triangle* by Sorosky, Baran and Pannor. These authors compared the surrender of a child to a "psychological amputation." They wrote about a deep sense of loss, pain and mourning that inhabits the psyche of all women who relinquish a child to adoption. This explanation helped to conceptualize my guilt, but I remained entombed in my emotional tunnel nonetheless.

For the modern reader, a woman hiding in the closet of unwanted pregnancy, fearful of acknowledging publicly that she has surrendered a child to adoption, may seem unfathomable. But the prevailing code of secrecy was real, and my growth from that terrified child and adult to the woman I am now is an evolution unexpected even by me. It is a monument to my belief that all aspects of our lives are created by us in order that we may grow.

This belief became another impetus for sharing my story. Could a seeming tragedy become a purpose in life, a vehicle for encouraging some design beyond the mundane? My hope is to transcend the surface, soap opera quality inherent in this tale and to awaken the repressed, lost child in all of us who hides in the land of secrets, shame and guilt.

1

Out of Childhood

We notice so often that what we imagine is exactly what we find.
—RICHARD BACH

I was born in Montreal, Quebec, of a French mother and an Italian father. Though programmed to please from the start, I never came close to the perfectionist model I fantasized.

As a child I learned that pleasing others gained approval; that being docile, subservient, never voicing displeasure, anger, fear or sadness pleased my parents.

My mother's behavior encapsulated the dedicated wife and mother. A brilliant intellectual, she mastered French, English and Italian, the latter two self-taught. When I was young she often played the piano. She wished her parents could have afforded lessons because she had wanted to become a concert pianist.

A small clue about my birth was revealed when I was almost seven. My mother and I had cleared the table after dinner. Neither of us spoke as I reached on tiptoe to grab a plate.

"I wish you'd been this quiet when you were a baby," my mother said as if talking to herself but loud enough for me to hear.

"Was I a good baby, Mama?" I looked closely as she reached into the hot, soapy water.

"Your brother Edward was a wonderful baby. He was always quiet. If he had been like you, I would have died for sure."

"What did I do?" My curiosity was replaced by a sense of shame for having been an obviously less-than-perfect baby.

"You were always crying and throwing up."

"How come?" My inquisitiveness pushed beyond my fear of knowing I had been bad.

"You were allergic to all foods. My breast milk made you throw up, as did every formula available at that time."

"How did I grow?" I remember asking that question as we both stopped working on the dishes.

"Well, the doctors had me soak flour wrapped in cheesecloth sacks in water. I boiled them until the liquid turned almost yellow. You were able to drink some of it and keep it down. Thank God your brother Edward was a good sleeper. You kept me so busy with your constant diarrhea." My mother continued with the dishes.

"How come I didn't die?" I handed her another dirty plate.

"We thought you might for a while. You only weighed fourteen pounds when you were a year old. But about that time you began holding down some food. Your dad and I were finally able to rest a little and we thanked God you seemed to be getting better."

"How come I was sick?" I searched my mother's face for hints.

"Doctors never knew. I think I shouldn't have had you so soon after your brother." My mother continued as if talking only to herself. "He was only eleven months old when you were born." She paused. "I didn't want you at first, but I grew to love you later on. I got pregnant so quickly after Edward."

"You didn't want a baby?" I had never before consciously wondered about being wanted.

"Not so fast after your brother. I felt ashamed after what my parents . . . oh, it doesn't matter anymore." She sighed deeply as she busied herself with the dishes.

I was not easily quieted, especially when every fiber of me was peeking into a hidden chamber.

"What did your parents say, Mama?"

It was an innocent question, but I held my breath and waited for her answer.

"They did not want me to marry your father and never attended our wedding. They did not like Italians, thought them all to be sex maniacs." Her voice was low again, almost a whisper.

"What's that?" I asked.

"Enough with your questions. Get me the rest of those dishes." I obeyed, knowing that our unexpected conversation was over.

Ours was a "proper" Catholic home. Religious pictures, statues and rosaries punctuated the surroundings.

"The communists will take over the world if we don't pray," my mother would often say.

Her attitude often echoed doom or disaster. I quickly concluded that if I prayed daily I would win my mother's favor.

By the time I started school, I wore a small bag of devotional medals attached to my clothing—each medal was a representation of the saints I prayed to throughout the day. Evenings ended with a private session of the rosary in my bedroom. I often attended daily mass when I was old enough to walk the few blocks to our parish church.

Even as a child I picked up a hidden agenda in the air, but I could never define or give it tangible substance. This mystery fed the beginning of my neurotic compulsions.

My room was so meticulously ordered that it seemed no one lived there. My grades were always flawlessly high, yet I felt "stupid" and a sense that I never did enough to be adequate permeated the very cells of my body.

Though my brother and I were chronologically close in age, we seldom shared our feelings. When we were both very young I can remember playing for hours with him in the living room, lining up hundreds of toy soldiers and horses with no more than ten words exchanged between us.

It is impossible for me to forget that during my early years constipation was my faithful companion. It might be argued that this was inextricably bound to my emotional tightness, but the only certainty I knew then was the recurring enemas. Today I assume they were ordered by the doctor whom my mother trusted, but no such explanation was given to temper the fear-saturated lens through which I peered at life.

On one occasion, I remember with perfect clarity sitting buttnaked on the kitchen table being prepped for an enema.

As I saw the plastic tube, I cried, "Put it in the other side. Please, put it in the other side," all the while pointing to my vagina.

"No, we can't put it in there," my mother and a visiting aunt yelled simultaneously.

"No, no, not there, please . . . please," I cried out feeling terror as well as shame knowing I was being bad by virtue of crying.

When my aunt held me down as my mother administered the enema, I sank into that deep, dark hole inside myself. This was the place where I could hold back fears, and my feelings were nonexistent.

My father was usually there but enemas were not his domain. When there were no people around to talk with he'd sit and devour several daily newspapers.

Though he never advanced beyond third grade he spoke four languages: English, French, Italian and Albanian. This fueled his socializing. He owned a neighborhood grocery store and this fluency allowed unconstrained conversation with the multi-ethnic customers. Crowds were his elixir of life.

My father's most loving communication centered around inviting people over for dinner. He was never happier nor more enthusiastic than when he was feeding friends and family. My mother expertly handled cooking for entire softball teams, while my dad charmed guests with his jokes. These dinners, as well as most family gatherings, were often the stage for my father's banter. Introductions to new and old faces would motivate my father to boisterously announce, "This is my daughter, Louise. She's got such small breasts that they're growing on the inside."

As people laughed at these jokes about my body, I would vanish into my inner sanctum where I felt nothing. I learned to expect embarrassment, and I would hold in my feelings to such an extent that I often felt I was hearing his words from a distant cave. This form of introduction became the most tenacious joke in my father's repertoire, continuing well into my early forties.

My mother stayed neutral when my father embarrassed me. She spoke to me once about coming to my rescue when the nuns at school made me kneel next to my desk for the entire day because they claimed I brought an indecent magazine to school. This accusation was not true—the magazine was brought by one of my classmates but the nuns did not believe me. I was not permitted to go home until I admitted to the crime. Obedient even in this lie, I finally said I was guilty. My release occurred hours after my classmates had already gone.

Once home I cried and told my mother what had happened.

"They're like the communists!" she screamed. "I'll tell them a thing or two tomorrow. Here I was worried to death when you didn't get home on time."

But she never went to school or spoke on my behalf, although I actually trusted that she would on this occasion. My mother's Catholic heritage would never have permitted her to accuse or censure a nun.

Her powerlessness became evident when she was suddenly whisked away to the hospital. I can only speculate that my mother's religious legacy diminished her ability to squelch my father's continuous jokes which often used us both as expendable targets. A dense soup of inner turmoil brewed inside her. I remember the words "nervous breakdown" were whispered by well-meaning relatives who stopped by with meals. I cannot recall how long my mother was in the hospital, but when she returned my ankle-length hair was cut because it had become too much trouble for her to care for.

My mother's illness strained our family life. Each time I attempted to engage in a friendship with someone my own age, she would take me aside and say, "I don't want you talking about our family to anyone."

The built-in absolute with friends was that I was never permitted to be alone with them. I never went to their houses nor walked home from school with anyone. My father usually picked me up at the end of each school day.

The taboo against intimate friendships peaked when I asked to join the Brownies, a Canadian version of The Girl Scouts.

"Those Brownies go camping in the woods and do all sorts of things you'd hate," my mother said when I showed some interest. Her disapproval stopped me solid.

The few friends I had who lived in the neighborhood were acquaintances at best. My father often compared me to them, the word stupid being the dominant theme of his "lessons." I know now that was his way of prying me out of my tunnel of shyness, but it did not serve me well. I never felt I measured up, no matter how perfect I tried to be. My life seemed a constant struggle to stay right side up.

2

Into the Cloister

You do not create your own reality. You create your own appearances.
—RICHARD BACH

Fear can be treacherous. Its menacing influence obliterates love on many levels. My spirit had been contained within its grip for so long that by the time my father spoke of moving to California, I had become such an expert at retreating into unconsciousness that I felt nothing.

I had long known that the Montreal winters were my father's enemy. He always spoke fondly of his native southern Italy, but for us to actually move away never seemed more than rhetoric. Yet the year I was fifteen, Edward sixteen, and my youngest brother Frank only seven, reality punched a hole in my protective shell. My father's ultimate dream took undeniable form when professional movers began to help my mother pack prized possessions. Many of these belongings were irreplaceable family heirlooms that were as much a part of her as her life's blood. Watching my mom send off her treasures forced me to recognize our imminent move.

Only when my assistance was requested, to help pack personal items, did I begin to picture California as a faraway land where the sun was always shining and the sidewalks were painted pink. My apprehension was inconsequential within the family structure, so as the final days approached, I withdrew deeper into emotional immobility.

When the time for that unalterable departure actually arrived, I obediently and quietly embarked. My inner misgivings did not subside for the entire week of our trip. They remained painfully high until we arrived at our rented house, and I saw the crates containing all the neatly-wrapped details of our "normal" back-home life.

Along with the concrete sidewalks and cloudy days which rattled my fantasies of the Golden State, all of my illusory dreams of social acceptance and a multitude of friends knocking at my door were quickly replaced by the reality of feeling isolated. As always, whatever I could not stand I internalized, and in order to escape my anxiety those first few days, I remained in a state of emotional stupor.

A week after our arrival in Orange County, I was enrolled in a Catholic high school. I quickly became the proverbial wallflower, the movie model of a shy girl. Team sports were anguish, and the glib social structure paralyzed me. My existing emotional alienation and malaise were compounded by this unfamiliar culture.

My only refuge lay in attending mass each Sunday. At least the church stayed the same. Here the priests were zealous about selling religious vocations, and they made it easy for me to channel my fears into a newly-defined mission to serve God. I decided to enter a convent school for girls who thought they had a calling to become nuns. This seemed a convenient place to hide, and my unconscious reward was a sense that I was pleasing my mother.

The Sisters of St. Joseph Convent was conveniently located near our home. It was an ideal, tailor-made escape. My father's philosophy was to not mess with such "callings," and my mother felt blessed by my decision. I sensed that she had often wished she had become a nun.

Ideally, a young woman enters the religious life to indicate her dedication to serving God. But my dedication was to circumventing public high school and the slippery unknowns of a fast-moving, unfamiliar culture. It was a deliverance that did not meet my vision.

Though long ago, I can still remember that first day at the convent. My parents delivered me to the front office, and a nun who looked old enough to be my mother's grandmother efficiently handled the admittance details. Our breath was audible, solemn, ceremonial. None of us spoke, contagiously absorbing the abnormal silence.

When the nun's wrinkled hand picked up my suitcase, her action communicated that it was time for my parents to go. They hugged me quickly and whispered, "We love you," as they left.

The nun waited at the foot of the stairway. "We'll put your suitcase upstairs," she said. She spoke softly, with a sense of finality that encouraged obedience. I followed her up the worn, wooden staircase.

Once upstairs, I stood in a huge dormitory whose shadowy chambers cloned repetitiously off one another.

"This will be your cubicle," she said pointing to one in the middle. "Put your things away and then return downstairs. We will join everyone for chapel prayers before dinner."

As I heard her steps echo on the stairway, I felt a sense of wonder as I looked around this space that was to be my room. It was no larger than a miniature walk-in closet. My necessities included a bed so small I breathed a thankful sigh of relief that I stood only five-feet-two. Five wooden drawers were partially opened, awaiting the friendliness of a few garments. Three hooks held clothes hangers. I had been measured the preceding week for the high school novice uniform, and I saw its green and white form, simplicity itself, efficiently hanging in its proper place. A heavy, brown cloth-like curtain pretended to be a door. The only uplifting thing, and it made me smile, was the tiny window. As I looked out at my view of the distant trees, I heard birds chirping. It would be only weeks before I began to envy their freedom.

Later, chapel prayers and dinner were comfortable enough as I easily acclimated to the rigid, ritualistic surroundings of convent life.

The predictability sustained me. We rose at dawn to attend mass, followed by a communal breakfast in the cafeteria. We attended classes, studied, prayed and participated in rotating chores during the hours before bedtime came around again. Neatness and order were long-time friends—mopping the floors was no better or worse than doing dishes.

Once a week after Sunday mass, we formed a single-file column of praying girls and walked around the gardens repeating the rosary. From here I could see cars driving past the convent gates—a window to the world outside. Over the months I found a longing growing in me to be driving away in one of them. They showed up my sheltered life as an unacceptable escape from a frightening world. I longed to be speeding away from the refuge that had become my prison.

I was beginning to feel that spending my life in silence, prayer, meditation or study was only an imagined escape from the anxiety of a threatening world. I began to concede that this life was tolerable only if I were to die and reap my eternal reward within a few years.

Never once did I discuss my confusion or fears with anyone. My other certainty was in knowing I could not die soon enough. A wise though uncommunicative part of me knew that being safe in this convent did not make me feel saved. Being there was, at best, a second-rate trade. There had to be something more. This hiding was a clever enough way to avoid what scared me, and yet I began to be frightened by the very fact of my hiding.

I decided I would leave at the end of the year. Though my parents visited me once a month and priest-confessors were readily available each week, I did not share my plans with anyone.

Although I could only guess what others thought, I noticed that the other girls my age acted differently than I did. They giggled and laughed more, and complained about the rules and not being allowed to sleep in.

I was astonished by and jealous of their carefree attitudes. Were they thinking of leaving as I was? I dared not ask anyone. They occasionally teased me about my compulsive urge to please, my high academic grades and my penchant for keeping my tiny cubicle fastidiously organized.

Looking back with adult eyes, I can readily recognize that this religious community awarded me many subtle gifts. I was exposed to hundreds of literary classics. Having never been introduced to any book of literary merit before, these novels stirred my imagination. They kindled fantasies of romance and adventure, a strange paradox considering I was there to hide from the world.

I also enjoyed the choir and received acknowledgment for my singing voice during my year's stay. I was surprised to be cast in the yearly fund-raising musical production, and this event brought forth an untapped part of me. Considered talented and intelligent, my participation in that play resulted in an unexpected endowment of self-worth. This strengthened my desire to leave the convent.

Towards the end of the year I announced my plans to leave. The nuns were shocked. I seemed to them to be the ideal recruit. I was aware of the inflexible canon that prescribed the protocol of an exit interview with Mother Superior. But when she called me into her office after hearing of my request I remember being frightened, thinking that somehow she would not allow me to leave.

Though so long ago, I cannot forget entering the large, austere office. I instinctively held my breath when I saw Sister St. Agnes sitting at her desk. She was the matriarch of the convent, a spiritual leader of sorts, our Mother Superior.

Before I had digested my apprehension and found even a hello her words snared me with their bluntness.

"If you leave the convent, you will follow the Devil." Her voice seemed to ricochet off the colorful, stained glass window directly behind her.

All my practiced scripts faded into penitent excuses. "But I don't have a vocation," I said.

"Sit down, Child, sit down," her voice mellowed, and I gladly sat in one of the two high-backed wooden chairs directly in front of the massive desk separating us.

Before I had taken a breath, she continued, "Christ will take care of you. He has called you to be his bride."

I felt pathetically inadequate, unable to find suitable words to express myself. Finally, I said, "I feel being a nun would guarantee my soul's redemption, but I do not want to live a convent life forever."

"You cannot turn your back on your calling." Her voice did little to relax me, and yet the chaos inundating my mind grew calm for a moment.

"Mother, I am sad every day. If I become a nun, I would do so only if I knew I would die within a few years so that I might secure my soul's salvation."

Silence filled the room, and yet I felt momentarily released from the direct order in Mother Superior's powerful eyes that dared to tell me I had to stay. Then with a valiant effort, this commanding woman stood up and continued her prayerful litany of persuasion.

"God has chosen you; this is your path. Leaving your calling will topple you into Satan's arms." Her words so tugged at my inborn desire to please that I instinctively sank back into my protective shell in order to block them.

"My child, we are all afraid. I have watched you this year and have seen you at prayer, singing God's praise and succeeding in your classes. You belong here."

In a reflex action, I uttered what I felt might placate her. "I have prayed for clarity, and my heart tells me to leave."

I knew she had not heard the plea in my words when I saw her mouth harden as her hand gripped the crucifix hanging around her neck. In that next moment she moved past me toward the door. Her heavy black habit and veil flopped up and down as she opened the door and motioned me out. She flung her final words across the room, "You will lose your soul if you leave."

Her wrinkled face was heavy and masked any trace of warmth. Words seemed futile at this point, so I left her office filled with anxiety. And although I dreaded the outside world, I left the convent at the end of the year sweeping the decree of spiritual doom into my inner void to reside with the collection of other traumas.

I never shared the why's of leaving the convent with my parents. They were not told about Mother Superior's curse. I sensed they were glad to have me back. On a spiritual level, my mother felt blessed to have a daughter with a religious calling. But when I returned home, she did not seem overly upset about that broken spiritual link.

My dad's religious convictions were typically European-Italian. He thought it his wife's responsibility to get him into heaven. Then, as now, he attends church routinely. He has an aggressive confidence that he will go to heaven and has never spent much time worrying about it. He had very little energy invested in my becoming a nun.

After my stint at the convent, I completed my last year of high school, graduating at seventeen. During that year I took a speech class and was urged by my instructor to enter a number of debating tournaments. I won many medals and trophies and received much-needed recognition. I discovered this to be another arena in which I could excel. But this acknowledgment came too late. The submerged monster of shyness and low self-worth lurked beneath the surface, like a dragon patiently awaiting release from its cave.

3

Out in the Real World

*Every person, all the events of your life are there because you have
drawn them there. What you choose to do with them is up to you!*
—RICHARD BACH

My first year of junior college was uneventful, except when a
dentist whose children I baby-sat trained me to assist in his office. I
worked late afternoons and Saturdays so that I could continue my
college classes. The money I earned was put aside for tuition and
books. Little did I know at that time that this private fund would be
ultimately utilized for something far different.

Though not in the convent, I was still tightly linked to the
Catholic church. Michelle, a girl I had met in high school and the
only close friend I had, was equally devout and continued a friendship with me after we graduated.

I learned that she had recently begun volunteering on a weekly
basis at a children's rehabilitation clinic. She read to children who
were physically impaired. I joined her, motivated by my respect and
admiration for her and my desire to work with young, handicapped
children.

The first time I went to the clinic I met Karl. He was the part-time
aid on duty those evenings Michelle and I were scheduled. He greeted us at the front desk.

"Hi, I'm Karl Cabigon, are you joining us?" he asked as he hand-ed Michelle her name tag all the while staring at me.

"Yes," I answered this young man with high cheekbones and dark, chocolate-colored eyes and hair.

"And you are?" he asked handing me a pen and name tag. I obe-diently printed my name on it as neatly as I could. He slipped it into a plastic cover, leaned over the desk and pinned it to my blouse. I wondered if he could hear my heart beating.

"The kids are in room twenty-three tonight, and they're waiting for you. Hope you've got some hot books," he said as he led the way.

"We've got some new ones. I'm sure they'll love these stories," Michelle answered.

Karl entered the large room with us. There were fifteen children there, most between the ages of five and ten. All were in wheelchairs and all seemed eager for personal contact.

We said hello to the children, split them into two groups and began reading. Karl sat and watched us for a long while. His warm smile melted any pretense of calmness I tried to display.

"Well, it would be great to watch you two all night, but I'd better get back to work. See you later." Once again he enchanted me with his smile before he walked out.

Michelle stopped reading and with a playful look in her eyes said, "He's never followed me into a room before. I've got a feeling he likes you."

"He's very nice," I said trying to catch my breath.

On our way out Karl stopped me and asked if I liked movies.

"Yes," I answered, captivated by this man whom I had just met.

"Want to go out this weekend?" Before I could find my tongue he continued, "There are lots of good movies in town."

"Sounds fine," I said.

"Give me your phone number." He put a small note pad in my hand and waved a pencil in the air.

I wrote my name and phone number on the pad. He looked at it, then I watched him put it in his shirt pocket.

"I'll call," he said as he walked down the brightly lit hallway.

"Wow, you two really hit it off!" Michelle seemed happy as we walked to the parking lot.

"Do you really think he'll call?" I asked, insecurity seeping through every cell.

"No doubt in my mind," Michelle answered.

Karl did call, and on our first date he met my parents. There was a brief introduction. Everyone behaved graciously. I was eighteen and other than occasional church-related social functions, I was out with a man for the first time on a real date. I felt important and valued.

As soon as I got in the car Karl asked me to move closer to him.

"My date always sits here," he said, patting the seat immediately to his right. I slid over towards him and he instantly put his hand on my knee. I felt a warm rush but said nothing.

When Karl's hand moved to my thigh, I was so bewildered by what I was feeling, and so consumed by an insatiable craving to be wanted and admired, that I anesthetized my uneasiness.

On the way to the theater Karl eased me into a more relaxed state of mind when he asked about my college classes. We exchanged details about ourselves. I learned he was nineteen and majoring in corporate business. During our conversation his hand never left my thigh, and I never shared about the convent.

We held hands in the movie and he put his arm around me. I was enthralled with these new feelings. When we returned to my parents' house he aggressively kissed me as we sat in his car. I stiffened.

He slowly pulled back and looked at me. "You have beautiful eyes," he whispered, "and irresistible lips." His words melted my uneasiness and I smiled. "Such a wonderful, lovable smile," he said, softly kissing me. Above all else I hoped my parents were not looking out at us. I took a deep breath and audibly sighed as his fingers lightly brushed my cheek. "You've never done this before, have you?" he asked.

"No," I answered self-consciously.

He laughed and said, "I'm gonna light your fire and you're going to love it."

He walked me to the door, sweetly kissed me on the lips and left me with the words, "I'll call you."

And he did. Every day he'd call for just a couple of minutes to say he missed me, and that he couldn't wait to be with me. I hungrily awaited his calls and I treasured his every word.

We dated every Saturday evening and my mother's inflexible midnight curfew was stringently obeyed.

On our fourth date, he stopped on a quiet, dark street a few blocks from my parents' house. He began kissing me with explosive passion, but when his hands found their way under my blouse I pulled away.

"You're so easy to love, so easy to love." He whispered the word "love" softly, hypnotically. The gentle look in his eyes disarmed my uneasiness. He moved closer, kissing my neck, but this time when his hand slipped under my panties I exploded into tears. Monster guilt had solidly welled up and grabbed me with its giant claws. Karl pulled away.

"Jesus, tears! Definitely something I've never experienced before at a time like this." His anger and sarcasm scared me.

My thoughts vacillated. I was desperate to be wanted and I was pushing the man who wanted me away.

Karl then momentarily stopped my tears when he said, "Listen, if you don't want me to touch you I won't, but I don't know how long I can be with you, and want you, and just hang out with kissing. We've been dating a month!" I looked at him, my face still wet with tears. "I'm taking you home." His words were riddled with anger.

A few moments later we were at my parents' house. He walked me to the door and left without even a hug. I felt shattered as I watched him walk away.

I continued my dental assistant job and my college classes but I felt empty and isolated. Six horribly long days passed before he called me.

"How you doing, sweetheart?" he asked as if nothing had transpired between us.

"I'm fine," I lied.

"You hungry for dinner tonight?"

"Yes," I said, my vision blurred with the joy of hearing his voice.

"I'll be there at seven. Can't wait to see my little angel."

Had I been able to step back at that moment in my life—had I been able to foresee the events I was about to create—I would have run shrieking until I found different, happier lessons. But, I did not run away. I kept my date with Karl, and that evening I stepped into a tunnel, and I did not notice the darkness.

We went to dinner, and afterwards he took me to his mother's house.

"Nobody's home," he said unlocking the front door, "My father has long flown the coop, and my mother works evening shifts."

Once inside, I met his dog. He played his guitar for me, and we kissed. I felt loved and accepted again.

Soon, he was unbuttoning my blouse and kissing my neck.

"It's time, my little angel," he whispered. "I love you. I know you love me."

"Yes, I do. I love you more than anything."

"Let me show you how wonderful love can be," he said carrying me to his bedroom.

There in the darkness he slowly undressed me, and when his naked body touched mine I was only aware of feelings I had never felt before.

I was more than a little lost in my tunnel, but I did not care. My overwhelming need to be accepted and loved activated me to abandon my religious convictions. Guilt paled beside my passion for Karl and my fear that saying no might send him bolting away, never to return.

I never associated intercourse with pregnancy. I had never heard the word contraception.

We continued seeing each other every Saturday night. The more time I spent with Karl the more I loved him, and the more time I spent in his bedroom the more I knew I would gladly have given my life for his love.

I stopped going to confession. A good Catholic confesses a sin only when there is an intention of never repeating it. I had no such plan. I could not conceive of never seeing Karl again.

I also attended mass at a different time than my parents. I did not want them to see that I did not receive communion. Receiving communion with an unforgiven mortal sin on your soul is a sacrilege. This compounds one's sin. It becomes a profane, blasphemous act. I was not ready to elevate the desecration of my soul to this level. I was willing to touch a mortal sin, but not a sacrilege in order to be loved by Karl.

Destiny wanted nothing to do with my religious doctrines. It was about to teach me a master lesson.

The lesson began a couple of months later when I missed my period and began feeling "different." I vomited several mornings in succession and felt nauseated or tired most of the time.

It would seem that my unconsciousness about the facts of life was prehistoric. Was it an arbitrary fate that had cast me in so unbelievable a role? I was flying upside down and little did I know then it would take me thirty years to land.

I did not mention my symptoms to my mother. My experiences with her did not include *tête-à-têtes*. But I did share my physical changes with Karl on our weekend date. We were in his car on our way to the theater. He became enraged.

"Do you know what that means? How can you be so stupid?" he screamed, as he recklessly began to speed. I held my breath, thinking he would kill us both.

"Shit! Shit!" Finally, he screamed, "You're pregnant!" Driving off the freeway to a less-traveled side road, he continued speeding.

"If you think I'll marry you, you're crazy!" He stopped and parked on a narrow dirt road. I began sobbing.

"I have two other children, a son and a daughter," he whispered. "I didn't marry their mothers, not even for my son. I'm not marrying anybody."

"Please," I begged, "I love you so much!" He lit a cigarette and inhaled as if it was the source of his power. Seconds later he started the car. I sat hypnotized by an inner panic.

"You've got to go to a doctor and make sure. Maybe you're not pregnant." Karl's words pierced the silence.

"I'll make an appointment with someone tomorrow," I said to soothe his anger.

"I'm not marrying you," he repeated.

Gravity seemed to intensify in an effort to squash my spirit. Mother Superior's words, spoken years before, echoed in my mind. That night, the Devil did indeed seem to have captured my soul.

Karl took me home, speeding all the way while I cried, feeling a cavernous disbelief that this was really happening. True to my word, I made an appointment with a doctor selected at random.

Paralyzed with shyness, I used my real name and address and told the truth about my marital status. A week later, at the follow-up appointment, I learned that the results were positive. The doctor offered no emotional or psychological help. If anything, I sensed a moral judgement.

"Do you know who the father is?" the doctor asked.

"Yes," I replied weakly.

"You're plenty early for no one to know if you get married," he said, looking at me with fatherly indignation.

I lowered my eyes, embroiled in my private shame. When I looked up, I saw him glance at his nurse with raised eyebrows as he walked out. She silently motioned for me to follow her to the front desk, where I paid for my test and visit. As I left the doctor's office that day, I felt a hollow terror. Once in my car, I sat shaking for a long while before I could drive home.

The fact of my pregnancy scared Karl so much that he stopped dating or calling me and never returned my calls. Countless nights, when I knew he was at work, I would drive to the parking lot at the clinic and sit crying in my car. When I saw him, I would beg him to marry me. Being pregnant would not have seemed so scandalous had he wanted me.

On those evenings, I'd tell my mother that I was going to the library. She believed the web of lies I wove.

After two weeks of my persistent presence and pathetic requests for marriage, Karl offered to arrange for an abortion. Perhaps he was beginning to suffer pangs of guilt. Whatever his motivation, the offer felt like an order. There was no dialogue between us. All power was snuffed out of me, replaced with a dark, all-consuming fear. Wrapped in confusion I stepped into his plan, hoping he would change his mind through some magic and marry me. My judgement was clouded with hopeless despair. Three feeble attempts to abort were made. The first time Karl drove me some forty miles from my home.

During the drive I quietly asked, "What will happen?"

"I'm not sure," Karl answered. "My friend said this woman could do something that will start a miscarriage."

"Who is it?" I whispered.

"I don't know, but it's only fifty bucks. You got the money?" he asked flatly.

"Yes, I do," I answered weakly.

If I had any mental pictures, it was of knitting needles being stuffed into me to cause bleeding. In my heart I did not want an abortion, and yet I felt powerless to alter the direction of my life.

Soon we arrived at a run-down neighborhood. Karl parked in front of a small, wooden house, which sat begging for a coat of paint. I felt sedated as I followed him to the door. An old Hispanic woman let us into the living room, where five people sat watching television. There were no pleasantries uttered. Everyone seemed to know why we were there. The woman stiffly gestured for me to follow her. I took one last glance at Karl, who looked away as he leaned against the front door.

Hypnotically, I followed this nameless person through a cluttered kitchen into a tiny, dark bedroom. She rummaged through a pile of moldy-smelling clothes and retrieved a long plastic tube. She said something in Spanish and pointed to my purse, pantomiming the counting of money. With a sour taste in my mouth, I took the money from my purse and handed her fifty dollars. Again she spoke in Spanish and motioned that I pull my pants down.

"Oh, my God," I cried as I looked into her deeply wrinkled face. She seemed impatient and spoke to me in Spanish again.

Convulsive sobs crumbled my facade as I bent over and pulled down my panties. With little hesitancy she began to insert the thick plastic tube into my vagina, while I recalled the enemas of long ago. Then, as she maneuvered her fingers into my body, I retreated into my private world until her voice jarred me into the moment. Seconds later she motioned for me to leave with her. Obediently, I pulled up my panties and followed her to the living room like a comatose robot.

Karl was waiting at the front door. Seeing me, he opened it and rushed out. I followed him, avoiding the glances of the people watching the small television. Trance-like and numb, I walked to the car where he waited silently. My thoughts were on the sensation of the plastic tube penetrating me.

"What is this tube?" I managed to whisper miles down the road.

"A tube? Oh, she did the tube thing," Karl lit a cigarette and inhaled deeply.

"Yes," I said. My mind was wrapped in chaos.

"Someone told me about that. Supposed to get air into the uterus and make it abort. Something like that," Karl said.

This can't be happening to me, I thought. Confusion surrounded me as I wept quietly, thinking I might die or that my baby might die. I wanted neither, yet I was losing my way in the narrow maze I had entered. Karl's words pierced my thoughts.

"Look, you're lucky I'm helping you at all. I never helped the others. So lay off the tears." Immobilized by his words, I coaxed my tears dry and listened to my heart pounding throughout the long ride home.

Once there I quickly slipped into my room, feeling overwhelmingly afraid of facing my mother. Riddled with the fear of not knowing when or how this tube would create an abortion paralyzed my sanity for a week. Absolutely nothing happened. Seven days later, with a surge of frail determination, I pulled it out. That things are seldom as they appear was evidenced by my continuing classes at college.

Only dimly aware of the emotional haze disorienting me, I returned to crying in the parking lot, waiting for Karl. He again rose to the occasion and solicited another woman to perform a similar style abortion. The following weekend, he drove me to a distant trailer park. A young Anglo woman met us at the door of one of the small, seedy-looking trailers. She seemed a bit hard around the edges but smiled a lot.

We had been there only a few minutes when she asked directly, "Why don't you have this baby and give it to me?"

Though timid and shy, her question stunned me. An inner voice pushed away my naiveté and warned me that this woman was not a suitable mother.

"Karl, you're a fine-looking guy and Louise is very pretty. You'll have a beautiful kid," she continued with her sales pitch.

I looked at Karl, who was smiling, his ego pleased with the compliment, and softly said, "No."

I was in precarious territory, but I genuinely believed this woman wanted to raise my child. Twenty-seven years later I was stunned after a friend read my first manuscript and quickly observed that this woman probably wanted a black market baby. I was unaware, then, of such sordid possibilities.

But, as I sat that day in the small trailer, this woman's words reunited me with the intense fear of having my baby. The only solution was not to be pregnant.

"We've got to move. Can you get going?" Karl's question quickly returned us to the matter at hand.

"Well, let's go, Cookie," she said, becoming the second nameless woman I followed into what seemed like oblivion.

We went down the tiny hallway into a bedroom. Only dimly conscious of anything but being a victim, I stood watching like a pitiful waif.

"Take your panties off," she ordered as she approached me with a thick plastic tube some five inches long. This reenactment of the previous experience melted any stoic pretense left in me. Weak-kneed, I leaned against the wall, sobbing.

"This won't hurt, Sweetie, relax," she said, trying to reassure me.

I pulled down my panties and focused on the flowered curtains. As I felt her fingers touch my skin, my tears froze while yet another tube was threaded into my body. Once again, I withdrew into my private world fleeing quickly through my secret doorway. I was safe there. No one had a key but me. There was no one there I had to please, and no one there I had to trust. There was only timelessness and a dark, soft cloud that I could dive into and hide.

"That's it, Kiddo, we're done." I heard her words from miles away and they returned me to the horror of the moment.

"Karl said you would have fifty dollars."

"Yes," I feebly answered while pulling up my panties.

I promptly located the money safely placed in my skirt pocket. Again, this was money earned from my dental assistant job. My body felt calcified and dense as we walked back to the dining room where Karl waited. He looked ill-at-ease and shot up the instant he saw us.

"Talk to you later," he said with a nod of his head, as I silently followed him out.

Tears streamed down my face during the ride home. Karl just groaned.

Returning home, I avoided my mother with practiced ease, and that week an impassive robot masquerading as me attended all my classes. As fate would have it, this attempt was a repetition of the first effort. Nothing happened.

Fearfully, I called Karl. Everything should have been complete, but it was not. I was spinning backwards. He felt my desperation and asked me to meet him at the clinic.

The following day, after my classes were over, I drove there and waited in the parking lot near his car. As his shift ended, I saw him walk toward me. His friend Joe was by his side. A heavy damp fog permeated the scene and reflected my mood. This encounter had an illicit flavor. I imagined police rounding us up for questioning about some transgression.

My car door opened as if by itself, and seconds later I was looking into Joe's eyes.

"Karl's been telling me what's coming down."

Karl slid in beside me and Joe leaned on the open car door.

"I got a friend in Tijuana. She's got connections. Karl said you'd go. You'll need three hundred dollars."

With a final desperate appeal, I turned to Karl and begged, "Please, let's get married."

"No! This is it with helping you," he screamed, turning away from me.

"Look, I can get it all set up for Saturday," Joe interrupted. "Can you be ready?"

"This is it, or you're on your own," Karl's voice cut through my indecision.

"I'll be ready." My words felt vacuous and foreign.

"Be ready at nine. I'll get directions from Karl," Joe said, shutting my door and walking away. Karl said nothing as he too melted into the thick fog with his friend.

I sat immobilized in the partially deserted parking lot for several hours and then mechanically retraced my path home. My future loomed grimly before me. Arriving home, my tangled web of lies supported me once more.

I withdrew more money from my savings, musing that this fund was supposed to pay my college tuition and buy books. Again a robot acted in my place.

Saturday came slowly. My mother believed more of my fabrications, as I left to seek an abortionist with Joe. This seemed a normal-enough day, and yet I was again the pathetic victim in a nightmare. The only power I could dredge up was to ask Joe to stop at a gas station because I felt nauseous.

I sensed that his friendship with Karl did not include my throwing up in his car.

"No problem," Joe said, looking at me.

A few more miles into this ghastly trip, I shared my biggest fear.

"Afterwards, if I'm hemorrhaging or something, take me to a priest."

Joe slowed down and touched my hand.

"If you were my woman, I'd marry you. You're the best Karl has ever had, but there was no convincing him to get married."

Genuinely touched by his concern, I whispered, "Thank you."

The ocean waves rolling by mesmerized me for a while, distracting my fears. But it became less and less possible to block the dense energy of Mexico, slapping me awake.

As we slowed down for the border crossing, we saw young children, only babies themselves, selling and pleading with sorrowful eyes, begging that we leave our money with them. They were experts at their trade, dressed in clothes screaming to be laundered, perhaps engineered to tug at visitors' pocketbooks. Everyone seemed to move in slow motion, as if in a dream. I had no feelings, except of being drained. I wanted to disappear or wake from my torment.

"Let's get something to eat," Joe said soon after we passed the crossing guards. "We've got time, we're early."

"I'm not hungry," I said, feeling nauseous again.

"Look, the person we're going to meet, she's at this restaurant. I'm hungry, so we can eat while we wait for her." This was the first time Joe's voice sounded edgy.

What I interpreted as anger so unnerved me that I quickly clammed up as he drove down several more streets, dodging barking dogs and the superficial glitter of tourist bait.

"That's the one! She's supposed to be there," he shouted, spotting a small cafe.

"You ready?" he asked, as he opened the door.

"Yes," I lied, as I got out and watched Joe lock his car. I walked past more brown-eyed children selling colorful blankets and tourist trinkets. Immune to anything but my emotional paralysis, I entered the cafe behind Joe.

We sat at a small table near the door, as Joe's eyes scanned the restaurant. With single-minded intent, he shot up and walked across the room to speak to a waitress. They appeared to know each other. A few seconds later he returned.

"No one's seen her today," he said, his whispered words heightening the subliminal evil of our being there.

"I want to go home," I whispered back to him from a strength seeded from a divine source.

"She'll be here," Joe insisted. "Relax, I got some food coming."

He seemed agitated again, drumming his fingers on the table. Then he caught the same waitress's attention with a wave of his hand. A friendly-looking woman, she smiled and quickly walked over to our table. Joe spoke Spanish to her. Being fluent in French, I could grasp some of the conversation. Their whispered words and furtive glances struck a chord of terror in me. I was afraid I'd begin crying in front of everyone if I heard the word "doctor" one more time. Luckily, with a final, hurried look in my direction, the waitress left.

"She gave me a name. We don't need that woman. We're home free," Joe looked pleased with himself and at ease once more.

Minutes later, another waitress brought food to our table.

I hung in eerie suspension for a critical moment. The insecure timid girl I was then battled with displeasing Joe. Wanting not to make waves and to do as I was told was etched deeply. I could not touch what he had ordered for me. So, I sat quietly and watched Joe eat.

I remember my mind reeling. How could I have intended to be so good and have actually been so pregnant? Then, for a microsecond, in my mind's eye I saw the tiny life inside me. This was my child! Instantly, I knew that no matter what Karl wanted, and no matter what the consequences, I could not kill my baby!

All one hundred pounds of me stood up and looked Joe directly in the eyes, "I don't want to do this. Please, I want to go home."

That clicked. Joe stopped chewing, looking no less astonished than I.

"Hey, if that's what you want. It's okay with me, either way." He sounded unbelievably relieved.

His eyes quickly scanned the restaurant. Spotting the first waitress, he got up and walked over to her. After a brief exchange of words and money, presumably for the meal, my eyes met theirs. I sensed an unexpected nonverbal communication of acceptance which deeply touched as well as surprised me.

"Let's go," Joe said, returning to the table where I had remained standing.

Within minutes, we were heading away from the fluorescent colors and heavy poverty, while I, perhaps for the first time in my life, felt consciously in charge of my life.

"You all right?" Joe asked after we had passed the border guards.

"Yes," I said, although I was not.

This newfound strength had recreated the reality of my being very much pregnant. The truth of my condition was now inescapable, and that terrified me. I wanted only to be hypnotized once again by the drugless escape of the ocean. Joe turned on some music and filled the space. The drive home could not have been long enough to suit me.

Juxtaposed with this memory, I recall a community where, fifteen years later, I incubated ten chicken eggs I found abandoned. Only two hatched. When I opened the unhatched eggs, I saw dead chicks in various stages of development. The sadness I felt generated tears for their loss. Now, remembering Tijuana, I am thankful that my courage emerged just in time. This life inside me was part of my cells, part of me. Fearful though I was, abortion would not have been a solution for me.

Arriving home late that night, I was met by my worried mother. On some level unknown even to her, she sensed danger. Her eyes reflected more than fear. Speaking in French, she asked, "Where have you been? Your father . . ."

"Mom, I've got to talk to you," I whispered, walking into the darkened living room.

I wanted the lights left off, but my mother turned them on as she followed me. If I had to confess that I had just murdered ten people, it would not have been as difficult as telling her my real secret. All my practiced lines abandoned me.

"I'm pregnant," I heard myself say. She looked incredulous. My father's snoring pierced the stillness, and I was temporarily soothed by knowing he was asleep.

"Karl?" My mother's question startled me.

"Yes," I answered, feeling relief that it was finally out.

"How many times did you do it?" My mother's Catholic heritage was her refuge, and it did not forsake her now.

With cosmic humor, I answered, "Once."

Soon my biggest fear was realized. Crying uncontrollably, my shocked mother woke my father while I sat motionless in the living room. He was being awakened into a nightmare, I thought. Were there a self-destruct button on me, I would eagerly have pushed it. I heard muffled sounds, followed by shouts of "stupid" and "gullible." Within seconds my father was standing before me, disapproval etched in his face.

"Will Karl marry you?"

A fair question, I thought. If only I could answer yes.

"He doesn't want to," I answered softly.

My father looked at my mother and with typical European-Italian certainty said, "He'll marry her."

My mother had stopped crying, but her face looked naked, reflecting shame and disbelief. Seeing her suffer pushed me deep within, where I went emotionally dead. My father's screams seemed to come from miles away. I remember my mother lifting my shell-shocked body by the arms as she walked me to my bedroom. As I prepared for bed, she quickly returned with half a sleeping pill.

"So you can sleep," she said nervously, twisting the ribbon on her bathrobe as her eyes filled with tears.

Early the next morning, I awoke to intense whispers. My parents were making some major decisions for me. For a moment their voices were still, as they left their bedroom only to continue talking in the kitchen.

Holding my breath, as if that would make me invisible, I quickly made my bed. Seconds later my mother opened the bedroom door.

"How are you?" she asked with genuine concern.

"Mom, I'm so sorry. I'm so sorry," I kept repeating as I sat on my bed crying.

"Your father and I talked it over, and we want you to quit your job with Dr. Parker and to drop out of school. We'll talk more after church. Why don't you get ready?"

"Mom, what will I say?" I felt powerless as I cried.

"We have to pray and be strong." My mother's eyes looked tired.

"Your father and I want you to tell Dr. Parker you have TB. Then he won't ask any questions and will want you to quit."

The magnitude and desperateness of this lie reflected the moral gravity surrounding my pregnancy. My mother's suggestion came from her heart and was said with all sincerity. At the time this did not seem any crazier than the reality of my being pregnant.

"This will work at school, too. They won't ask any questions if you're sick."

"I can see a counselor and Dr. Parker on Monday," I answered obediently.

"Get ready for church now," my mother said, getting up from the bed. Then she turned and whispered, "Remember, your pregnancy will always be our secret."

My mother's words, "will always be our secret," alerted me for the first time that she never wanted anyone to know I was pregnant. How was she imagining hiding the fact when I began to show or when my baby was born? On that day, I buried the dilemma of keeping my pregnancy a secret and when my mother closed the bedroom door, I only felt the irrevocable reality of a child inside me.

Age has sowed some seeds of wisdom on my path. The adult I am now believes we write mystical daily scripts in order to learn our life's lessons. Looking back on the girl I was then evokes the image of a mouse caught in a maze. And that mouse did in fact go to school on Monday and tell a counselor that she was dropping out because she had TB. The counselor was incredulous.

Pulling my file and observing my excellent academic record, he said, "You're too smart to let this get you down. I want you back here next semester." Shaking my hand firmly, he smiled and said, "Take care."

A cadaver would have had more clarity than I had that day. When I arrived at work and told Dr. Parker my story, he seemed equally stunned.

"TB, huh?" He was an old dentist, and I avoided his glance. "When did you find that out?" he asked.

"An X-ray, a few days ago," I said, still the proficient liar.

"Don't want you to stay then. Talk to the front desk about your check. They'll have your hours." His smile looked forced.

Could he have guessed? I fearfully wondered. There was no cheese for this mouse at the end of the maze. There was only a circular, living darkness.

Arriving home late that afternoon, my mother met me at the door.

"Did you tell them?"

"Yes, I talked with a counselor and with Dr. Parker. My last check will be mailed to me, and I'm officially dropped from all of my classes."

"That is best," my mother said. "Now go look in your room; I have something for you."

Full of nothing but the sense of my own limitations, I walked into the bedroom. There on the bed was a thick corset. My eyes met my mother's.

"You've got to wear this in case anyone . . ."

"Mom, I'm not showing," I interrupted.

"A precaution," my mother picked it up and handed it to me.

I began wearing it. Can a corseted mouse ever find the way out of its maze? It was symbolically heavy and stiff, not unlike my thoughts.

Later the next day my best friend Michelle stopped by to say hello. I walked out to her car to create some privacy.

"I didn't see you at school today."

"I've dropped out," I quietly said.

"Why? You're doing so well."

"I'm pregnant," I said, not knowing where the courage came to share my secret.

"Oh, God, that's why you stopped volunteering at the clinic! Now I understand." Michelle was stunned. "What are you going to do?"

"I don't know," I answered honestly.

"Is it Karl's? Yes, of course, it is," she said, answering her own question.

At that moment, I felt more sorry for myself than guilty, but my lack of clarity did not allow me to see whether or not that was an evolution in consciousness.

"Do your parents know?" Michelle asked, leaning on her car.

"Yes."

"Will you get married?"

"Karl doesn't want to," I said, noticing my mother at the front door. Her body and gestures motioned me in.

"I've got to go," I said nervously.

"Let me know what you do," Michelle anxiously whispered, eyeing my mother.

I walked to the door, where my mother waited as Michelle drove off.

"Did you tell her?" There was fear in her question.

"Yes," I answered, knowing I had just compounded my sin.

She grabbed my arm and pulled me inside.

"No one is to know. Don't tell anyone else. Promise me."

I nodded like an obedient child, instantly doubting my trust of Michelle. My parents' fear was contagious.

"Your dad and I went to talk to Karl's mother earlier today. She did not know or would not say where he was. Dad was going to force him to marry you. He's a coward. I hate that man."

My parents' detective work on my behalf rendered me speechless. I had never seen my mother so angry.

"You went to talk to Karl?" I finally said, feeling a need to confirm what I heard.

"He's taken off, his mother does not know where he is. He's a coward! A coward!" She angrily repeated the word, as if to verbally do him some damage.

By the end of that day I had capitulated—I wanted to do whatever my parents requested of me. Perhaps I was partially satisfying a need for atonement. In bed that night, I imagined the cliché of clichés, a shotgun wedding. I wondered if Karl's running away was worse than what lay ahead.

Not knowing what else to do, my parents went to the Catholic Social Welfare Agency. There it was suggested that I be hidden so no one would discover I was pregnant. During the sixties, Catholic agencies spent their energy hiding the pregnant girl in a "wage home," so that society would not judge her.

In such a home an unwed girl worked as a live-in maid and baby-sitter in exchange for a place to hide while she was pregnant. A monthly stipend of approximately fifty dollars was paid. This money was often sent directly to the agency and the girl never saw it. This simple procedure delivered an abundance of babies for adoption purposes. I was in the tightly locked box of a well-oiled system and my confusion allowed nothing but blind obedience.

4

Down to the Depths

The mark of your ignorance is the depth of your belief in injustice and tragedy.
What the caterpillar calls the end of the world, the master calls a butterfly.
—RICHARD BACH

At least now abortion was out of the question. But no one offered me any other options, or discussed the possibility of my keeping my child as an unmarried woman. No one at the agency ever spoke to me about my dreams, hopes, fears or my future. All decisions were made by my parents and the welfare bureaucracy.

The agency functioned like a controlling business director. I had written a script as victim, and I played the part flawlessly. Never once did it occur to me to request decision-making power or even to suggest I be provided with alternatives. Never once did it occur to the Catholic Welfare Agency to provide me with choices. Their job was to process babies. My naiveté, guilt and fear played easily into their deceptively benevolent, protective arms.

My parents quickly embraced the dehumanizing wage home plan. They were also not counseled nor given options. I was to be shuttled out of public sight like a potato buried deep in a root cellar, awaiting a later time when it can be utilized.

The following week I was driven to my hiding place, my refuge and my prison. Each of us was overwhelmed as we headed into precarious territory. I was docile, obedient and quiet throughout the fifty mile trip. My mind played host to guilt and fear.

Arriving there, the house seemed ordinary enough. It stood next to other conventional homes.

"This is it," my dad said, as he got out with my suitcase.

My mother and I followed him silently. I tried to convince myself that this was best, as we walked to the front door in single file—my dad in front, me in the middle, and my mother following us—like birds flying south for the winter.

Someone had heard us drive up, and the door opened before my father's hand touched the bell.

"Hello, I'm Mrs. Ross," a young woman smiled and led us inside.

"I'm Dario and this is my wife," said my father. Five young children watched from the dining area as we walked in. "And this is Louise," my father finally said, completing his introductions.

Mrs. Ross left for a few seconds and returned with another pair of eyes. This one she carried. We were introduced to the baby and the other five children.

"Nice family you have," my dad said diplomatically.

"We'll take good care of her," Mrs. Ross quietly said, as she led my mom and dad out. I saw my mother's eyes fill with tears, as she stole a last look at me standing like a waif amidst five children. It seemed like I was an outlaw holed up at a hideout.

"Are you going to be here long?" one of the children asked.

"Seven months," I said, looking into a pair of blue eyes.

"Everybody out to the back yard. We'll call you in for dinner soon." Mrs. Ross's order scattered the gang, which ran noisily outside.

"You can put your things away later," I was told, as she gestured for me to follow her into the kitchen.

There on the table was a formidable pile of clothes begging to be folded. Following her example and wanting to please, I began folding clothes.

"What am I doing here?" I thought. "You've been very bad," my mind answered. If only my cunning mind could have helped me vanish.

Later that evening, I met Mr. Ross. His work hours were long, and our paths seldom crossed other than when he drove me to church. I soon learned to diaper the baby, assist with dinner, clean the house and help put six children to bed.

My room was upstairs. It was small—a sanctuary of solace. Every evening I said my rosary and prayed for forgiveness, before I fell asleep.

My shyness precluded much intimacy. Functioning on automatic, I attempted to be the perfect domestic help, hoping that somehow this effort might nullify my sin. There was always housework to do or children to care for. Leisure time did not exist, since I was raised to please and liked order. Early in my stay I did some reorganizing.

One day when Mr. and Mrs. Ross were out and the children were asleep, I formulated a closet system in which the smaller children's personal items were easy to reach and methodically arranged in a visually attractive, yet workable scheme. *Ladies Home Journal* would have been ready for a photo layout when I finished reorganizing the linen closet as well.

"Who did this?" Mrs. Ross inquired of me the next day.

"I hope it was okay," I responded with some fear, thinking that I should not have changed anything.

"This is amazing. I'd been planning on some sort of order for the kids' closets. I just never got to it. Thank you so much."

Mrs. Ross was genuinely pleased and certainly surprised.

It is only recently that I learned Mr. and Mrs. Ross followed a pledge to keep an emotional distance. The lack of camaraderie or vulnerable sharing during those seven months was not totally attributable to my shyness. They were never told my last name, nor did they ever ask. It was believed that if they learned more about me on a personal level, my pregnancy would have been exposed.

My own two brothers and relatives in California were told I had gone off to a distant school. They each accepted the lie and bought into the deception. Reality was miles away.

My mother would visit me once a month and drive me to St. Anne's, an institution for unwed mothers in Los Angeles. These monthly trips were an opportunity to get out of the house, much like a prisoner on temporary parole. The California freeways were torture on my mother, but my inability to be philosophical about my situation overwhelmed any possibility I might have had to recognize my mother's anguish.

Once at the hospital, she was required to wait in the car. How could she explain her presence if someone she knew caught sight of her? She slumped in the car seat and wore dark glasses just as I did. We never spoke of our discomfort. The shame and fear of the experience could have been a potential gift if it had led us into genuine intimacy. But we were both emotionally disabled, light years away from authentic sharing of our feelings.

Concealment was practiced at all levels. The rationalization for this furtiveness was that I was being protected. On my first visit a nun checked me in as Louise A., as last names were never used. She then ushered me into a small cubicle and instructed me to change into a hospital gown. Soon another nun dressed in a starched white habit led me to an examining room.

"Have you been to confession?" she asked, as I walked beside her.

"Yes," I answered, feeling like an advertisement for lust and sin. A nurse opened a nearby door and motioned me in. Once inside she helped me onto the examining table, positioning me so that my feet were in the stirrups and raising the gown to my waist. As the doctor began his unexplained and unanticipated probing between my help-less legs, I started crying and my knees visibly shook. No one had thought to explain a gynecological examination to me.

"Doesn't she have pretty eyes?" the nurse said, attempting to comfort me.

All efforts to calm me failed. The procedure was mercifully short, but later in the dressing room, I felt violated, ashamed and deceived. An assault of tears became my only defense. I never shared my embarrassment with my mother—instead I was numb and quiet on the ride back to the wage home.

Some time into my pregnancy, realizing that no helpful communication occurred at my monthly hospital visits due to my shyness and the fact that I was always greeted by a new volunteer doctor, I asked my mother to bring me a book about pregnancy. I wanted to become familiar with the changes in my body. In her paranoia she refused, believing that if she borrowed or bought such a book someone would make a connection between my absence and her purchase.

The first movements of my baby within me awakened me to tears. As my body changed, I struggled to understand the metamorphosis.

As I began to show, the few maternity clothes I needed were purchased by my mother at a store some fifty miles away from where she lived. The one time my father came to visit was to drive me to San Diego for a haircut. The beauty shop was over one hundred miles from the wage home. As if to emphasize the phobias and guilt and in order to protect me from accidental discovery, I was given special permission by the local Catholic bishop to attend weekly mass at six o'clock on Friday mornings, because there were less than a dozen people at this service. Though Mr. Ross drove me to church and attended the mass with me, we seldom spoke beyond the perfunctory pleasantries. That this pregnancy was to be hidden was compellingly obvious.

During that time I expected a social worker to call me. Such a visit had been promised, but no one ever spoke to me about it. I felt disembodied, circling somewhere above my life. When would I be allowed to land?

Years later, I learned that my girlfriend Michelle had been invited to my parents' home for dinner. She was threatened that if she ever told anyone I was pregnant, she would be killed! We were all victims. Continually immobilized by my deficiencies, my delivery reflected the labyrinth in my mind. I was in labor ten hours before I told Mrs. Ross what I was experiencing. When the pains began early that morning, I thought I was sick. The sensation was much like menstrual pain, so I made no connection with labor. My baby was not due for two weeks—once again I attached no relevance to my body's signals. Never having discussed this aspect of pregnancy with any of the doctors or nurses I saw at the hospital, I was ill-prepared to recognize what was happening. The price of shyness, guilt and fear was high.

Around 9:00 p.m. my pains were beyond denial, so I went downstairs to tell Mrs. Ross that I felt sick. She quickly grasped that I was in labor and called my mother.

My bag packed, I anxiously waited by the front door as Mrs. Ross sat with me.

"Just breathe and relax. Everything will be fine," she said as kindly as I had ever experienced her to be.

One hour later my nervous mother arrived. Within seconds my suitcase and I were whisked into the front seat, doors were slammed shut and the car roared towards Los Angeles as if swept into a recondite mission.

The wreckage in my mind and my mother's fears on the Southern California freeway at night with a daughter in labor created the same atmosphere as if we had had a time bomb ticking visibly away in the car.

Only once my mother asked, "How are you doing?"

"I'm fine, Mom," I answered, not knowing if I really was or not.

When we finally arrived at the hospital, we both sighed with relief. Walking side by side through the darkened parking lot heightened the undercurrent of gloom that engulfed us.

As I stepped to the door and knocked, a nurse opened a window on the second floor and shouted, "What do you want?"

"I think my baby's coming," I answered.

"You were supposed to call first," she screamed and shut the window.

Once again, I had not followed the acceptable script. Once again, for the thousandth time I had proved myself unworthy of love and approval. Once again, my efforts to please others and avoid their anger had failed. I feared the nurse might not let me in.

It seemed like an eternity before a light came on inside the darkened doorway. Seconds later a nurse opened the door. She looked grim and stolid.

"How do you feel?" my mother asked, as we both went inside.

"We'll take care of her. You need to leave," the nurse interrupted. She reached across and took the suitcase from my mother.

"You'll be fine. I'll come tomorrow, if they let me." My mother's eyes filled with tears as she turned to leave.

Left alone with a nurse not all that happy with my presence pushed me deeper into fear, while the rigid Catholic obedience permeating the air fed my penchant for emotional withdrawal.

"Well, we might as well check you over since you're here," she said, as I mechanically followed her into a small room.

"What's your name?"

"Louise Antognoli." I spelled my last name for her before she asked.

"Put this on and lie on the bed," she ordered, handing me a hospital gown.

I was left to change in the brightly lit room. A few minutes later the nurse returned, reading some notes from a folder in her hand.

"Probably a false alarm. You're not due for two weeks." She kept reading while I wondered if I'd be sent back, though I did not ask the question.

"You're nineteen? You don't look over fourteen," she said in disbelief.

My mind weighed whether it was any less horrible being pregnant and not married at nineteen rather than at fourteen.

Shortly thereafter, I was prepped for the doctor's inspection, and then following a painful contraction, my water broke.

"I'm sorry I'm making such a mess."

"Never heard anybody apologize for that before," the nurse laughed.

My contractions were close together now, and the pain was more intense. Still, it did not seem appropriate to cry out, so I gritted my teeth and instinctively took a deep breath. It is not easy giving birth while wishing to be invisible, but that seemed my only bastion of protection.

Soon a doctor arrived, checked my progress, and called for the nurse to get me into the delivery room.

"Looks like this is it," she said, wheeling my bed out of the room.

At 2:55 in the morning, my daughter was born. The doctor looked at me and said, "I hope I don't see you in similar circumstances, ever again."

After he left, the nurse held up my baby, showing me twenty tiny toes and fingers. I extended my hand and briefly touched her little foot, whispering, "She's mine."

Not wanting to prolong the agony, the nurse quickly wrapped my daughter in a blanket and disappeared from sight. Left alone amidst the sterile artificial brightness, I could no longer sustain my stoic facade. Tears welled up like ocean waves, unleashing the empty, wounded mass I had become.

Then a nurse arrived and rolled me back to a small room. Neither of us spoke. She seemed in a hurry. As she left, I recalled my childhood fantasy of raising and loving a child. Out of reach, my dream was replaced with a grief beyond description. I have never before or since felt so afraid and alone. The question, "What have I done?" reverberated in my brain.

Hospital rules dictated that I stay for five days. My mother could not visit, but each day I was allowed to see my daughter for five minutes. Though naive and uncommunicative about my needs, I mentally wondered why they were allowing such visits. Didn't they know I was not permitted to keep her? The bond between us grew each time I saw her. She was unbelievably beautiful, not wrinkled like newborns are supposed to be. The nurses called her Dimples because hers were so deep.

I struggled to understand my position in this game. Seeing her each day was the cheese at the end of the maze, but some animal instinct warned me that this was whimsy. The tunnels I traveled were clouded with uncertainty. I was having trouble sleeping and found myself sobbing uncontrollably a good part of each day. Nurses, nuns, doctors and hospital workers walked past my room, but no one ever talked to me. Wishing to be invisible had made me so.

On the third day after my daughter's birth, a nun came into my room.

"Please sign this," she said, putting a paper on my lap.

"What is this, Sister?" I asked, looking at what seemed like an official document.

"This will give us permission to baptize your daughter." She was calm and pointed to the empty line marked "Baby's Name." Under that line was a space awaiting my signature. It did not occur to me to challenge this request. The walls of my maze were crumbling under the steely gaze of the nun. Every moment of the pregnancy had paved the way for giving up my baby. Imagining names eroded what little logic I could dredge up. The meager strength I possessed collapsed.

"It is not uncommon for an infant to suffocate in its crib. You must protect the immortal soul of your daughter," she said, putting a pen in my hand.

I signed. The ink was black. An instant name, "Julie Marie Cabigon," arose clearly from somewhere in my muddled mind. I took her birthfather's last name. Is that legal? I wondered, but did not ask.

"Thank you, Dear." The nun folded the paper and left.

A few moments later, another nun stuck her head in my room and said, "Come with me."

Quickly grabbing my robe, I followed her down the sterile halls to the elevator. Its small enclosure held four young women, each holding an infant. One of these was my daughter, who was so close I could have reached out and touched her. "Grab her and run for your life," my mind screamed. Instead, I focused on her dimples. The elevator jerked into motion as I began to sob uncontrollably. Embarrassed, I wanted to either disappear or gain some semblance of composure in front of these strangers. But no one seemed to notice. Perhaps my sadness was accepted as atonement for my sins.

The elevator stopped. The door opened and, still sobbing, I followed the procession into the chapel. A priest waited at the altar. We inched up to him, one behind the other. The nun directed me to stand to the side, and the girls holding the babies were motioned to stand next to the priest. Holy water was symbolically sprinkled on each tiny forehead, while the priest uttered prayers requesting absolution from original sin for safe passage into heaven.

When her turn came, my daughter's cries joined in sad unison with my own sobs. This mournful harmony fully linked me with my baby, as our cries ricocheted off the vaulted ceiling and stained glass windows.

Suddenly the nun gestured, and the girls with the newly baptized infants streamed out of the chapel. As quickly as I was whisked from my room, I was returned to it, still weeping. I sat on my bed, aching for some clarity. None came.

The next day the invisible arms of bureaucracy sent another messenger to my room. Camouflaged by polite amenities, he was the ultimate surgeon. Permanent separation was imminent.

Early on the last day of my stay in the hospital, he walked unannounced into my room, introduced himself as Mr. Thomas and proclaimed he was my adoption caseworker.

"Well, Louise, we have a few papers you need to sign before you leave today." He did not waste time in getting to the matter at hand.

"We need to ask you a few questions. Just answer as best as you can." He sat on the chair next to the bed and removed a thick folder from his attaché case.

I wondered who the "we" were that he spoke of. I felt angry.

"What are these papers?" I ventured to ask.

"These will help us find the perfect family for your daughter," he replied matter-of-factly.

"The adoption papers?"

"You can call them that," he continued. "Let's see here. Your ethnic background?"

"I'm French-Canadian on my mother's side and Italian on my father's."

"Do you know the father's background?"

"Yes."

There was a cloud of puritanical sanctity blanketing this question. "He is?"

"He's half German and half Filipino."

"Are you a high school graduate?" he asked next.

"Yes, I'm a sophomore in college, and my daughter's father is a junior in college." Surprising myself, I added, "And I get straight A's." This unsolicited information was hostile. I wanted this man to know that my daughter was not only genetically predisposed to beauty but also intelligence. This baby, who was secretly being given away, was mine. Flying blind in this whole process, I ached to have a guarantee that her placement would be flawless. The questions asked by this stranger seemed so shallow and inadequate.

"Do you or anyone else in your family have major medical problems?"

He interrupted my anger, and I returned to the docile victim role, bent on pleasing and doing as I was told. "On my father's side, there have been several uncles who died of heart attacks."

With this I stopped, realizing a tenuous balance existed here. I wanted to tell the truth and yet was fearful that less than a perfect history would mar my daughter's chances of being adopted. As the white spaces disappeared on Mr. Thomas's forms, I realized the inked-in words represented my daughter's potential as someone else's child. Nevertheless, I felt anything but honesty would be an injustice to her, so I continued with the truth.

"On my mother's side there has been some cancer. I personally have never had any medical problems."

"And the father?"

"I don't know about his medical background."

"Do you or the father have any special talents?"

"I've been told I have an excellent singing voice. My father and mother both have pleasant voices. My dad plays the guitar, my mother the piano. My daughter's father plays the guitar."

"You should have a very musical child here." He smiled and filled in more spaces on the form.

"That about does it. We need you to sign right there." He pointed to a fresh white space.

I took his pen and signed my name, inking in the last space. Methodically, Mr. Thomas put the form into his attaché case, shook my hand and left.

Alone in the room, I felt like my daughter and I had been vaporized, condensed into simple questions and answers. The reality of our separate journeys flashed before me. She was to be procured by the agency, and I was to be buried in a maze.

No more than a minute later, a nun stepped into my room.

"Get yourself packed. Your mother's on her way to take you home," she said, leaving as quickly as she appeared.

Her words jerked me into consciousness and ambivalence. I wanted to mourn or escape but did nothing.

I filled the time by obediently packing my suitcase. Sitting on the bed, I listened to the sounds of the hospital and wondered if I would see my daughter one more time. No one came.

Then I heard my mother's voice. Her distinct French accent filled me with a sense of anxiety. A nun escorted her to my door.

"Are you ready?" the nun asked.

"Yes," I answered and looked at my mother. Her smile did not completely mask her sadness.

"Daddy's waiting in the car," my mom said, picking up my tiny suitcase.

We walked past the desk where each month I had signed in as Louise A. The nun left us alone.

"Everything is taken care of," my mother said, noticing that I looked around for permission to leave.

On one level I knew I was leaving a secret behind, but as I passed through the heavy wooden doors, no rationalization could come close to healing the psychological wounds I carried in place of my little daughter.

Crossing the parking lot, I saw my dad waiting in the car.

"Hi, Louise." He started the car the moment my hand touched the door.

Once on the freeway I melted into the back seat. I knew I did not have to "hide" anymore, and yet I did not want to be seen. My mom sat beside my dad. A somber mood filled the space as we took off.

My dad broke the silence.

"We will all forget this. No man will ever want to marry you if you tell."

His pronouncement reflected the rules of society written by judgement and inherited through fear. Ignorant of the consequences, we felt a need to continue weaving a tight fabric of lies, but the agency had not prepared us for this part.

"No one knows. Everyone still believes that you've been away at school," my mom said, obviously uncomfortable.

"I won't ever talk to anyone about it, I promise." I wanted to stop the churning in my head.

"Everything will be fine. You'll start school again next month, and your life will be just like before." My dad was serious.

We were so naive. I felt emotionally maimed, as I sat there pretending secrecy would cover up the wounds. The story we wove on the trip home was fantasy. In reality the secret would never be buried, yet the plan seemed to work on a surface level. My two brothers were glad I was back from school. No one asked what school I attended or where it was or why I was returning in mid-

August. Everyone was conveniently unconscious. My mom and dad and I acted our parts well.

A few days later, I received a letter requesting my presence at the welfare agency. I arrived at the appointed time. Mr. Thomas greeted me.

"Hello, Louise." He motioned me to follow him into an office.

"We have one more paper for you to sign." He pointed to a neat white sheet on his desk.

A surge of anxiety overtook me as I picked up the pen placed directly next to the form.

"Right here," he pointed to the correct spot. I signed my name. "Are you okay?" he asked me. Did he notice my hand shake? I wondered.

"Yes," I lied, having no skills to communicate the chaos in my mind.

"Your daughter is a special needs child, but we will find a suitable placement." Mr. Thomas put the paper I signed into a cream-colored folder.

"Special needs?" That phrase hurled me into fear.

"Because your daughter is one-quarter Filipino, she is a little more difficult to place."

"You will find a good home for her?"

"No problem," Mr. Thomas said, getting up and walking to my chair.

"Thank you for coming today, Louise."

I got up, shook his hand and left. I was filled with misgivings and apprehension, yet voiced nothing. My questions drowned in a mass of shame.

A surge of tears poured out as I drove my car randomly around town, not wanting to go home. The only comfort I could imagine was a church, so on that late afternoon I found myself sitting in the last pew of a darkened sanctuary.

Some rebellious urge moved me to take a photo from my wallet. It showed me as a girl of ten, standing on the balcony of our home in

Montreal. My long dark hair was loose and ankle length. Slowly on the back of that snapshot I penned:

Julie Marie Cabigon

August 7, 1961

7 lbs., 7 oz.

19 ¾ inches

Los Angeles, CA

Born 2:55 A.M. Monday

That photo is still in my wallet.

As the flickering candles lit the plaster statues, I held the picture and sobbed. The words "She's mine" flowed with each tear.

5

After the Wreckage

*There is no such thing as a problem without a gift for you
in its hands. You seek problems because you need their gifts.*
—RICHARD BACH

When I attempted to contact Michelle, a few weeks later, I learned that she had entered a cloistered convent. Our lives were to touch again, but not for several years.

There are times when I think of Michelle and myself as cosmic twins. Her life has carried her through a short period in the convent, to marriage, to infertility caused by endometriosis, to adopting a son and authoring a book. Even her time spent living in different places has been inconsequential to our friendship. We have never lost touch with one another and can always pick up where we left off, as if we communicated daily.

After the birth of my child, I regretted Michelle's inaccessibility, but my conscious hours were completely filled as soon as I re-entered college.

Two and a half years later I earned my B.A. and three teaching credentials. Still shy and quiet, I kept my secret safely stuffed in the inner recesses. Though I had been on the published honor roll for many semesters with a 4.0 average, I felt stupid, and never felt I was doing enough to be accepted or loved. No one expressed enthusiasm about my having completed college. I did not attend the graduation ceremony. My diploma was mailed to me. A veneer of high grades, diplomas and credentials did not begin to touch the inadequacies that long ago had melted through my innocence to possess my core.

During my last year in college I met Bob, a brilliant intellectual. There was little warmth or romance those few months we dated. The words "I love you" were never spoken by Bob, who believed this expression was overused and trite. The woman I am now would not be attracted to him, and yet I married this man.

A deep desire was that, once married, I'd get pregnant and this child would be mine to keep. But fate did not support my dream. I worked as a teacher for the entire four years we were married, while Bob earned his master's degree.

Our life together revolved around his criticism and ridicule of me. He was often away, working on theatrical productions at the college. Bob's main interest in life was his participation in intellectual conversations with friends.

Remembering that period of my life flings me into a time warp. Though I was the breadwinner, fear and guilt eroded my ability to play any part but that of victim. Verbal and emotional debasement constantly punctuated our relationship.

I never revealed to Bob that I had a daughter. That was my own, personal secret, crammed together with guilt and regret in a private Pandora's box. I knew of no reward for consciousness. I was unaware of the damage my silent fears were reaping. Countless nights I would wake crying and then shuffle to the living room to seek seclusion. That scene seldom varied during those four years of marriage.

I was always on the losing side when I communicated a need for Bob to say "I love you" or to help with the finances. There was no contest between us. Fear that he'd find out about my secret put me in a constant state of apprehension.

I had believed torment lived only in nightmares. But Bob had two close friends who spent a great deal of time with us and their presence, coupled with Bob's, was torture for me. Paul and Sandra's critical opinion of me, which my lack of self-worth prompted me to believe, stuck like hot glue to my senses.

One weekend after they had recently moved to a community a few hundred miles away, Bob wanted to visit them.

"I don't want to go," I said as he prepared to pack.

"What's the problem?" Bob looked stunned.

"It's too far," I lied, knowing that the truth was unmentionable.

"It'll only take a couple of hours to get there. Paul and Sandra are expecting us. Come on, get packed."

"No, I'm not going." Where I dredged up this courage to disagree dumfounded me.

"Do what you want. I'm going," he shouted angrily.

Bob went without me. Sitting alone in our apartment, I listened to my mind scream, "Escape!" A piece of my world was crumbling. I was back in my maze, but this time I would jump over the wall. With little thought, my heart beating loud enough for me to hear, I raced around the apartment and grabbed a few personal articles, leaving all household items and furniture. Throwing this small collection in my car, a tiny sense of exhilaration peeked through my anxiety. Knowing that I had all I needed to survive, I locked up, got into my car and drove off.

I know now that there was little power in my behavior, but there is no question that I could have left Bob any differently. A "twilight zone" quality is always evident when I look back at that time in my life.

Seeking refuge like an escaped criminal, I found an apartment near where I taught. It was a small, inexpensive place, but it provided a hideaway. The barren rooms strained in their emptiness while a vacuous senselessness swelled in my gut. Sleep and hunger eluded me, but being alone provided a measure of safety.

I discovered later that when Bob returned and did not find me home his worry took a back seat to his anger. This fed his decision to not attempt to locate me. When I finally called him, I was unable to explain my behavior to him or myself.

My invalidation machine was running full-steam. Self-awareness and self-trust were unlikely partners for my guilt. A primitive instinct in me feared that if I were to see Bob he would drag me back and lock me in the prison that was our marriage.

Bob's only effort to save our marriage came when, during a phone call, he said, "I don't want to become a divorce statistic." Perhaps if had he said, "I love you," I might have stayed.

Leaving all the possessions acquired in our four years of marriage and paying in total for the divorce seemed a small price to pay for freedom. My conscience was only slightly relieved by the expense.

About this time I began having many physical problems. I developed persistent endometriosis, the same disease that afflicted Michelle. My monthly menstrual pains became unbearable due to uterine tumors. Even with pain medication I often could not teach. My periods lasted ten to twelve days with heavy bleeding between cycles. I took various drugs and hormones, none of which alleviated the disease.

Basically, my reproductive organs no longer functioned. The recognition of the psychological ramifications of disease stemming from the emotional paths in our lives is not new. It fit for me. When the lining of the uterus sloughed off, and tumors formed on my intestines and bladder, doctors performed a total hysterectomy, removing my uterus and ovaries. I recall feeling that this was a punishment from God.

My daughter was never far from my mind. Each year there were more birthdays, more Christmases and more questions. "Is she okay?" "Is she happy?" "Is she alive?" I never secretly stopped looking into the eyes of young girls my daughter's age wherever I went.

Leaving Bob had given me a small feeling of confidence. Living by myself in that tiny apartment felt safe. My parents were deeply saddened that I had divorced. They kept asking me why but there were no reasons to appease their sadness. I'm not certain I had a reason. How do you verbalize an avalanche of fear? I was still so buried under my past that I could not be accurately analytical about any part of my life. Living alone for a few months was a welcome change. It was the first time that no one was around to criticize or laugh at me. I felt safe.

A few months after I left Bob, I met a fellow teacher's friend and fell in love. Not unlike most women in the early seventies, I was deeply frightened at the prospect of living alone for the rest of my life.

Paul was a lot like my mother. He was quiet, somewhat insecure and extremely intelligent. Of major importance to me was that he and his circle of friends were into therapy. Many of them were in group therapy or saw a therapist individually once a week. Paul was in such a group. He explained that therapy presented the prospect of helping people shed their deep-rooted anxieties and fears. I inhaled this information like someone breathing in air after being rescued from a cave-in.

Anxiety was still a constant companion to my guilt. I was not eating much and consequently became very thin. Friends would ask me what was wrong. Telling them would have required being introspective, revealing my secret and confronting my sense of imperfection. I had no tools with which to do that.

My daughter was six at that time and always floating in and out of my thoughts. My extreme need to be perfect was at odds with the reality of divorce and the surrender of my baby to adoption.

All the talk about therapy pushed a button of hope. Seeking relief from my anguish, I decided to sign up for a weekend retreat for couples. For one hundred dollars I would experience group therapy. I lit up like a Christmas tree at the thought.

When I shared my enthusiasm with my parents, they resisted this new avenue in my life.

"You want to hear that we were bad parents, is that it?" My mother was plainly worried.

"You don't need to talk to strangers about your life." My father's comment was pulled from his own private maze of fears and judgement.

Though I'd been stopped by less opposition many times before, I found the strength to go ahead with the group experience. Privately, I wished I had not mentioned my plans to my parents. Paradoxically, I continued to want their approval, but I did not want my eagerness squelched.

The weekend held its own lessons. The retreat was a cardboard semblance of my hoped-for deliverance. Fate cunningly annihilated my grandiose fantasy of instant clarity, strength and self-worth attained through therapeutic osmosis.

What I experienced instead was my silence, fear and inability to trust. Most of the people there were couples, but a few like myself were single. The large comfortable room in the mountains offered a safe place for those present to gain insight, but I remained silent. It was an agonizingly long weekend.

Returning home, I felt drained and painfully aware that I had not escaped from my maze. Therapy seemed to offer only a minute possibility for me. My Pandora's box had not been cracked. I felt doomed to hide alone, holding hands with my secret, feeling powerless, lacking confidence and believing myself to be stupid.

A revelation came when I remembered the others at the retreat. Many had gained clarity. I could not understand then the power of trusting and sharing, but I was no longer lodged as deeply in the mire of my swamp. I learned that those who had shared the most plowed doggedly through their muddled lives. They had talked. That was the catalyst. Perhaps I could confide in someone and learn to cope with my remorse.

Feeling like a dreamer, or perhaps drunk with newfound hope after my therapy weekend, I felt compelled to trust Paul with my secret.

One evening while we were discussing music and he was playing his guitar, I blurted out, "Do you think if you found out something bad about me you'd still like me?"

"Something bad?" Paul smiled.

"Well, something no one knows about me," I continued, checking every nuance in his reaction.

"You robbed a bank?" He put his guitar down and waited for me to go on.

Was I as pathetic as I thought myself to be? I wondered, looking at Paul. Like a convict being released from prison I walked through the clanking gate of fear by saying, "I had a baby six years ago."

"You had a baby?" He was perched on the edge of his chair.

"When I was nineteen, I had a daughter." There, I had said it. My entire being was condensed into those words.

"Where is she now?" Paul was more curious than shocked.

"I was told she was adopted by a good family. I don't know for sure." My hands shook and I began to cry.

"That's what you were afraid to tell me?"

"Yes. How can a man ever care for me knowing I had an illegitimate child?" I continued to weep, feeling bottomless regret.

"Do you see me running out of here?" He took my hand.

"You don't mind?"

"There's nothing to mind. I don't see you any differently now than I did ten minutes ago. I'm sorry for you, that it happened the way it did." Paul seemed as mellow as usual.

I looked at him and felt bound in a powerful way by what I had shared.

"I don't want anyone else to know. Don't . . ."

Paul interrupted, "I have no need to mention this to anyone."

"Thanks for understanding." I had taken a great risk. Having faced my fear, I knew that a great chunk of it had melted away. Paul knew my secret yet still loved me. Would others be as understanding? For the first time I felt that my secret was not as vile as I thought.

"Want to go over that song we're learning?" Paul asked, breaking into my thoughts.

"Fine, let's do that." I wanted to short-circuit the sadness I felt when I thought about my daughter.

Paul and I had begun to rehearse and build a repertoire. My first attraction to Paul had been his talent on the guitar. My singing experiences at the convent had fed a desire to sing to an audience, and it surfaced again when Paul and I first began singing at parties together. That happy beginning quickly mushroomed into nearly one hundred polished songs, and we auditioned at local restaurants and clubs until we landed a job. A great measure of confidence emerged when I sang. It temporarily satiated a bottomless hunger for love and approval.

We worked together on a small scale for two years until the entertainment arena was no longer enjoyable. Continuous auditions and problems with getting paid for our performances were non-ending chores, and singing in smoke-filled rooms was a physical drain. When club owners insisted I dress more provocatively, I felt it was time to quit. By then singing had lost much of its fascination.

A few months after we ended our short musical adventure Paul and I were married. But the events of my own life were overshadowed by thoughts of my daughter. She was eight at the time. I had looked into the faces of thousands of girls who had her coloring, her dimples. My guilt was bound in layers of regret that cast a shroud of remorse over me. A ceaseless reverberation of questions haunted me. Is she in a good home? Is she healthy? Does she hate me? Doubt cultivated a strange climate in my life. My thoughts were always clouded with my phantom child.

Life with Paul was gentle enough. Though often passive and quiet, emotionally uncommunicative and depressed, he did not rip me with criticism or ridicule, and he had a wonderful sense of humor. One night some eight years into our marriage, we had some mutual friends over to dinner. Unexpectedly one of them began sharing a story about a woman friend who had been looking for her mother.

"She's been looking for years. Last week she felt so close. Then it turned out to be the wrong person."

"Is she an adoptee?" I was hesitant to believe it was so.

"Yes, she is."

"And she wants to meet her birthmother?" I was almost shouting.

"She's been looking for ten years."

I could not have imagined hearing more miraculous words.

"How old is she?"

"She's around thirty."

"She's been looking for ten years?" I whispered the words. Everyone at the dinner table looked puzzled. Only Paul had a clue to my behavior.

As I sat there an invisible seed of courage suddenly became fertilized and inexplicably grew with science fiction speed. It was an instantaneous emergence from a dream state.

"I'm a birthmother," I revealed, opening the door to my secret closet.

"Really, Louise?"

"Yes, I surrendered a daughter to adoption sixteen years ago." I was overflowing with long-buried strength. "I don't know where she is or how she's doing."

Would she ever want to look for me? I wondered silently. My thoughts took me far from the dinner table. For the first time, I poured concrete energy into the bottomless desire to meet my daughter. For the first time, I gave myself permission to openly think my questions.

"Louise, I'll have Betty call you. Would you mind that?"

My friend's voice brought me back to the present.

"I'd love to talk with her."

In that moment, I began to create my miracle.

Betty called the next day. She was a sad woman of mixed ancestry who was still desperately searching after ten years. Closer to her goal and more optimistic than she had ever been, Betty's life was intricately orchestrated around finding her birthmother. She was the first to actively draw me out of fear and hiding into an awakened state. She was my introduction into a society I never dreamed existed.

The Search

I learned from Betty about an organization call ALMA, Adoptee's Liberty Movement Association. This is an organization created by Florence Fisher, who successfully completed a twenty-year search for her natural mother in 1971, and then placed this ad in the *New York Times*:

> *PERSONAL*
> *Adult who was an adopted child desires contact*
> *with other adoptees to exchange views on adoptive*
> *situations and for mutual assistance in search*
> *for natural parents.*

Her intention was to reach other adoptees seeking to fill the vacuum that keeps them from their past. A deluge of letters poured in from all over the country.

Today, ALMA is the largest organization of its kind in the United States. Their slogan: "The truth of his origin is the birthright of every man."

I began attending monthly group meetings in San Francisco. Betty's single phone call propelled me at lightening speed into the vortex called the adoption triangle. I was out of my maze, and my Pandora's box was open wide. With high-powered, purposeful energy, I left my self-imposed imprisonment behind.

Soon after attending the first meeting, birthmothers who were strangers called to share their sadness and guilt. My number was lighting up the phone wires. There was no time to judge the appropriateness of stepping out of my closet. I was out.

The monthly meetings in San Francisco introduced me to hundreds of adoptees and birthmothers. Meeting and talking with others on my wavelength was powerful. These kindred souls understood my grief, regret and sadness. I found an outlet for my private, secret guilt.

ALMA meetings included search workshops at which adoptees who were at least eighteen traded experiences and discussed the problems, adjustments and conflicts of looking for a birthparent. This "age of majority rule" applied to birthparents as well, and since my daughter was only sixteen at that time I received no help in a search. I attended these meetings to hear about reunions and to talk with adoptees and other birthparents.

At that time, I decided to send a nonidentifying health history to the adoption agency who had handled my daughter's adoption. I learned that it was legal to send such information. Should an adoptee or adoptive parent request these facts, assuming they've been sent, they are shared, though all identifying specifics, like names, are never revealed.

Suddenly, it occurred to me that I did not know the name of the agency who had handled my daughter's placement. I knew that the Catholic Social Welfare Agency had processed my daughter through some bureaucracy who handles placing children with hopeful adoptive parents. But, I was never told which agency had supervised these arrangements. I had never asked and no one volunteered that information. I wrote the Catholic Social Welfare Agency and request-

ed this information. They wrote back telling me that these files had
been lost.

Encouraged with visions born of television fantasy I went to a
detective agency. At that time this seemed like a logical plan. The
four hundred dollars I spent accomplished nothing: the agency that
had handled the adoption could not be identified. I sat in a messy
office with pock-marked furniture and listened to the dead-end
report. There was a soap opera quality to the proceedings, as if I were
a participant in a grade B movie.

With few options open to me, I continued attending ALMA. At the
next meeting, I was introduced to an organization called CUB, Concerned United Birthparents. In The Birthparents' Perspective, I read:

> *In 1976, Lee Campbell and three other women in Massachusetts
> met to discuss their experience as surrendering parents. There it
> was decided to pursue the formation of a group both to explore this
> unresearched phenomenon and to support the rights of adoptees to
> obtain their birth history and birthparents' identity. Lee began the
> work contacting other birthparents known to her through her
> involvement in an adoptee activist group and through readers of a
> Boston newspaper's column. Other meetings were arranged, and
> the incorporation of the nonprofit group was effected in October of
> 1976.*

I learned further that this group does not help in searches.
Rather, it provides emotional support for birthparents. CUB believes:

> *The feelings and needs of the birthparents are real and legitimate.
> They have been ignored, belittled and suppressed too long under the
> guise of protection! Birthparents are the givers of life and love and
> desire not protection but the opportunity to perhaps one day extend
> the hand of friendship (as is allowed anyone else) to their birthchild,
> as one adult to another. The birthparent has no wish to rival or
> threaten the relationship with the adoptive parents; it is well known*

that adoptive parents are the "real" and "true" parents in the most meaningful sense. They only want to eventually know the end of their story, and this is surely a right as valid as those of the adoptive parents of an adult. It should be remembered that the birthparent relinquished all rights as a parent, but never gave up the basic rights of a human being.

Today, there are twenty-five hundred members of CUB spread across the nation.

"Humanizing adoption" was the phrase that stirred a desire in me to start a CUB chapter in Sacramento. Insight gleaned through the years has led me to believe that thoughts are things, and at that time in my life I was fired with a determination and persistence that was as deep and powerful as any force in the universe. This was the time of gestation for my miracle: my thoughts were single-mindedly centered on finding my daughter.

I decided to list my maiden name and phone number in various phone directories of large cities in California. If my daughter were ever to look for me, these listings might help.

KFBK in Sacramento generously allowed me to tape weekly public service announcements concerning CUB. The announcements educated listeners as to the purpose of this organization, gave the date, time and location of the meetings and publicized my home phone number.

Desiring even more information, I began to research adoptions in North America. I was shocked to discover that there are millions of adoptees in the United States. As I write today, there are five million people—one out of every forty—who have experienced this condition. And I had been thinking my situation was unique!

I organized and led CUB meetings in my area for over a year. During that time I met several hundred birthmothers and five birthfathers. This is not to imply that men are less sensitive to their offspring—it is that the birthmother's physical bond is so much stronger. The sexual double standard is undeniably prevalent, but talking with the few birthfathers I met led me to understand that their sadness and guilt were felt no less severely. It is not surprising that many birthfathers have never allowed their sadness to surface, since our society has long encouraged emotional restraint in men.

Interestingly, many of the women who attended the meetings were physically fragile. Some spoke of hysterectomies at a young age. Diabetes, thyroid problems and kidney problems were not uncommon. Fifty percent of the women who came to the meetings had created disease in their bodies. Criticism, anger, resentment and guilt accompanied them in thought and action.

"No one ever counseled me regarding keeping my child," one fifty-five-year-old birthmother shared.

"All the misleading advice I received when my daughter was born was manipulative, all devised for me to surrender my baby," another woman painfully detailed during one of the meetings.

"My parents wanted nothing to do with me when they discovered I was pregnant. I was condemned. Today, when I permit myself to reflect about the daughter I gave up, I find the grief excruciating," a forty-year-old spoke up.

"There's not a day that goes by that I do not think of my birthson. Through the local social welfare agency I spent the final months of my pregnancy hiding in a wage home. Working there was sheer drudgery. Currently, I wonder if I'll ever meet my son." Sharing this, Barbara, who was forty-five, began to weep.

There were many tears shed at those monthly meetings. What became obvious was that few had allowed themselves to grieve, and none had come close to touching the regret and guilt they felt. A relentless remorse occurs when someone's energy is focused unremittingly on guarding a secret rather than learning to forgive and love themselves. A social support system to help these women was lacking at that time. The CUB meetings broke down the barriers so that the experience of sadness might lead to healing.

These women were between the ages of twenty-five and sixty. Some never came to the meetings. Many called me at home, afraid of attending a public group.

"I don't want my husband or children to know that I have a son I gave up to adoption thirty years ago. I just wanted to thank you for starting that group. It's a good thing." A woman who called shared her fears with me.

Attempting to help her resolve her guilt, I said, "If you could attend one meeting and talk with others like yourself who were scared at first but have learned a measure of self-confidence in telling the truth, you might . . ."

"No. You don't know my husband. It would be too hard." Her voice shook.

"I hid in the closet for sixteen years. It is difficult to step forward, but it can be done." I was powerless to ease her fear.

"I just wanted to thank you, that's all." She hung up.

I had read about ex-convicts who committed murders and were less reluctant to divulge their past. Is a surrendered child parallel to murder? This secrecy was severely handicapping families, and it was needless. This woman's call was one of many that pointed to lives of quiet desperation and emotional congestion. Most were hungering for the opportunity to someday meet their son or daughter.

CUB and ALMA meetings became my life's blood. Each time I met another adoptee searching for his or her birthparents, my own desire was deeply validated.

Through my association with these organizations, I learned that it was my legal right to know whether my daughter had really been adopted—I was beginning to have serious doubts that she had. I also had a right to know which agency handled the adoption, and some general facts about the family who adopted my daughter as long as their identity was not revealed. I wanted that information.

On a whimsical hope of discovery and armed only with my health history, I drove to St. Anne's, the maternity hospital for unwed mothers, where my daughter had been born. My single-minded zeal propelled me through my fear of the Los Angeles free-ways, and eight hours later I walked through the same heavy wood-en doors that I had exited sixteen years before. There at the front desk I faced a nun.

"May I have a tour?" I blurted, realizing immediately how stupid this request must sound.

With a shocked look on her face the nun replied, "No, this is a private hospital. We do not give tours."

Startled into reality I said, "I had a daughter here sixteen years ago."

The nun's face softened. Moving to the front of the desk, she sur-prised me. "Things have changed here since then. Perhaps I can give you a quick tour." She motioned for me to follow.

Walking silently behind the long black habit triggered a sense of mourning for my daughter. I instantly remembered my monthly vis-its, and I began weeping uncontrollably. My mind circled again. I wondered why I had come here. Suddenly, as we walked down a long hallway a grey-haired man emerged from a room.

"This is Mr. Adamson, our hospital administrator." The nun smiled politely. "This is a young woman who had a child here years ago."

"I'm Louise Jurgens." I offered my hand, still weeping.

He lit up with a big smile and seemed unaware of my tears.

"Please stop by before you go. I'd love to visit with you," he said, returning to his office.

Feeling like a nefarious celebrity, I went on a Cook's tour, visit-ing places I had never seen before. Dredging up a stoic resolution, I calmly walked in and out of the hospital cafeteria and delivery rooms.

The nursery was empty except for one tiny infant. Ten or more unoccupied cribs offered up their starchy white comfort. I wondered when infants would fill these empty cribs. I hoped none ever would. As my peripheral vision caught sight of the infant for a last time, I saw the agency as consciousless—the taker of a mother's child to give to a stranger.

Our last stop was the chapel. Was it a masochistic need to suffer that drove me through those doors? For a single moment I hesitated and then followed the nun. From a cellular vault located deep inside myself, I retrieved tears buried long ago. I stopped in the center of the aisle, unable to move closer to the altar. Painted saints and stained glass windows stared at me while a curtain of baptismal memories fed my tears.

"We have to go now." The nun's words pulled me back to the present moment.

"Mr. Adamson will be waiting."

"Yes, thank you, Sister," I whispered and followed her out.

The hospital administrator was indeed waiting.

"How are you? Have a seat," he gestured as I appeared at his door.

I sat down in front of his opulent-looking desk. The nun disappeared without a word.

"I seldom get to talk to anyone years after they've been through these doors," he said, sitting behind his desk.

"What brings you here after all these years?"

"I'd like to know how my daughter is," I stated honestly. "I've never been certain she was really adopted. I want to send a non-identifying health history. Might that be possible?" I was afraid of sounding less than articulate.

"There's no reason for you not to know that your daughter was adopted. What was your daughter's birthdate and your name then?"

I gave him the information, and he wrote it on a slip of paper. He got up and walked to a large file in the corner of his office. My eyes followed him. Does he have anything for me? The long-familiar maze constricted around me as I waited.

Minutes later he returned to the desk with a large file and began flipping through the pages.

"The Infant of Prague Adoption Agency handled this case. Your daughter, being one quarter Filipino, was considered a special needs child then, and this agency had the best prospects for placement. This is information you have a legal right to know. If you contact this Fresno agency you could acquire some nonidentifying facts about the family who adopted her. You might also give them your health history." He spoke softly and slowly, looking at me all the while.

I felt calm as I wrote these pertinent details in a small notebook.

"Do you have other children?" he asked.

"No, she is my only child."

"May I ask how you are employed?"

I felt a vestige of righteousness attached to his question.

"I am a junior high school teacher," I told him.

"I appreciate your efforts in coming here today. Your request seems harmless enough. Good luck in your endeavors."

Mr. Adamson stood up. I understood that my interview was over. He walked me to the lobby door, and we shook hands.

Never before had I felt such hope. Within the next few days, I made an appointment with a social worker at The Infant of Prague Adoption Agency, which was located several hours drive away in Fresno, California. I shared my "find" with the CUB members, who were happy for me.

On the day of the appointment I dressed conservatively so that I would make a good impression, realizing again how much of my life I engineered to please others. Wearing a tailored grey suit and black pumps, I drove south for several hours until I reached Fresno. I felt eager and full of expectation.

The building seemed innocuous enough. I half expected the dispenser of my daughter to be cloaked in black. The secretary at the desk directed me to a chair.

"Are you Louise?" she asked.

"Yes."

"Barbara will be with you shortly."

Within a few minutes a young woman opened the door to an office and motioned me to come in.

"You're Louise?" she asked, extending her hand.

"Yes."

"I'm Barbara. How are you?"

"I'm fine. Thank you for seeing me."

"How can I help you?" She sat down at her desk.

Wanting to be precise and clear, I thought for a moment before answering. "I surrendered a daughter to adoption sixteen years ago and I've never been certain she was really adopted."

"Was the adoption handled here?" Barbara asked.

"Yes, the administrator of St. Anne's in Los Angeles recently told me that the adoption was handled through this agency."

"Sixteen years is a long time ago. We do not maintain a file for that length of time." She looked concerned as she spoke.

"I want to send a nonidentifying health history, if that's possible," I said.

"Let me see what we've got."

Again my name and the date of my daughter's birth were exchanged.

"I'll be right back." Barbara left me alone in her office. Muffled, rustling paper noises from the adjoining room stirred up sadness. My confident energy seemed to disappear, and tears began to flow with each elapsed minute.

When Barbara returned she was empty-handed. My heart skipped a beat. What had she found out? Was there no record?

"Your birthdaughter was indeed adopted," she said, sitting down. Her words helped me leap out of my doubts.

"Her adoptive parents had three natural children and a fourth who died soon after birth. The mother could no longer have any children."

I breathed deeply as my eyes filled with tears. An uncontrollable surge of sobbing stripped away all illusion of composure. My sadness seemed unbounded. Barbara handed me some tissues.

"I feel like a part of me was wounded many years back, and I am just now feeling it," I whispered through my tears.

"There have been many tears shed in that chair. It might help you to know that this family wrote many letters to many adoptive agencies throughout the state requesting a child, preferably a son, as they already had two daughters and only one son. They realized they were low on the priority list because they had their own children and were not wealthy people. Ultimately your daughter, a special needs child, was given to them." I continued to weep.

"Are you all right?" Barbara asked with genuine warmth.

"I'm sorry I'm crying," I replied.

"It's okay to cry."

"Do you think I can ever meet her someday?" I asked.

"The structure of existing laws will only allow me to send a non-identifying health history, and that is assuming I can locate this family. The address I have is sixteen years old. I cannot communicate any other details."

Momentarily transported to the time of my daughter's birth, I saw my tiny, five-day-old baby being given to this faceless family.

"I will get back to you when, or if, I locate the family."

Barbara's words awakened me to the moment's reality. She stood, handed me another tissue, and then walked me to the front door.

"Thank you for your help." I offered my hand and left, still crying.

The return drive was clouded with memories and generously layered with sorrow and guilt. Some of my grief had atrophied, but talking with Barbara had removed the sedation of time, and my sadness became a reopened wound.

As soon as I arrived home, I recorded the day's excursion in my journal and then wrote to this young woman who had the power to contact my daughter's parents.

Dear Barbara,

Meeting and talking to you a few hours ago breathed a breath of life and warmth in the previous cold travel which led me to the Infant of Prague Adoption Service. After more than sixteen years of doubt and fear I feel a measure of comfort in knowing for certain that my daughter was indeed adopted and is in a loving home. Your sensitivity and genuine kindness with regard to my interests and concerns are appreciated more than you can imagine. Many thanks for your help. My thoughts are with you as I wait to hear from you in the near future concerning your efforts on behalf of my daughter and myself.

Sincerely,
Louise Jurgens

My work with CUB kept me busy. As president of the Sacramento chapter, I was offered the opportunity to investigate current bills dealing with adoptions. CUB was actively involved in promoting legislation facilitating an exchange of information between an adult adoptee and birthparents. In the late seventies, such bills always provoked intense and emotional controversy. They sparked an explosive debate much like the abortion issue, raising questions worthy of the wisdom of Solomon but nonetheless left in the hands of legistators.

In 1978 Senate Bill 535 would have changed the rules, making it possible for adult adoptees to get in touch with birthparents, if both agreed. I researched this bill and sent an article to *California Journal* titled, "Shades of Solomon." It was published in their August issue and I became a "free lance writer."

I continued to check my mail each day, eagerly hoping to hear from Barbara. My need to be doing something led me to write a screenplay loosely based on my personal experience. My life had become open to the possibility and need for miracles. Why not one more? I fantasized that my screenplay would be produced, and information concerning my daughter would materialize and help me locate her.

I wrote a screenplay entitled *Marcie*. Script in hand, I drove to Los Angeles, obsessed with my plan. I had acquired a few names and phone numbers from local agents. With these as armor I entered a war zone. My journey into this strange and foreign territory was a colorful adventure. Even with my naiveté, I escaped unscathed.

About this time my weekly public service announcements began to spill into requests for interviews on local radio and TV stations. One of the major newspapers in the area also called. I passionately believed my daughter would recognize me through this media exposure. Thinking about this now, I can only marvel at my idealistic vision. My daughter might have lived anywhere in the world for all I knew, and she did not know who I was or what I looked like. Yet, an incontrovertible trust that I would find her through the media never faltered.

Finally, my compelling need to hear from Barbara at the Fresno agency was realized a month after our meeting. My hands shook as I read her letter.

Dear Louise,

> *It was nice to talk with you, and I am glad if I could provide you with a more complete sense of resolution to your feelings. I did locate the family who adopted your child. First by phone, then in person. They were very appreciative of your concern and the obtaining of the medical information. The adoptive mother is very proud of her adopted daughter. She has grown to be a beautiful young woman who is bright and happy. She said her health has been unusually good, but she was still glad to have the information should she need it. I removed all identifying information on the material I gave to the family for confidentiality reasons. I hope everything is well for you. I really enjoyed visiting with you, and I also appreciate the long search you have made to provide this infor-*

mation to your child. Please let me know if I can help you further within the very confining aspects of the law at this time.

> *Sincerely,*
> *Barbara Ellis*
> *Director of Social Work*

Upon reading the letter countless times, I knew I could not settle for anything less than talking with Barbara one more time. The thought of sitting in a room with a person who had talked to my daughter's mother was irresistibly enticing. I made an appointment for the following week.

Driving down on the appointed day, I was more nervous than I had been the first time. The agency held the winning hand. They called all the shots in this game. I wondered if there would be a few cards left for me. Would I discover my daughter's first name, or the city where she lived? Such questions obsessed me as I drove. My automatic pilot navigated the freeway to the agency while I calculated my prospects for success.

As I walked into the front office, I heard my heartbeat as I wiped my sweaty hands. I felt I was walking into a secret, hidden cavern. With the hopefulness of one younger than my thirty-five years, I sat optimistically waiting to see Barbara.

"She will see you now," the woman at the front desk said, as she walked to open what I remembered to be the door to Barbara's office.

"Thank you." I entered and stared at the only person I knew who had seen my daughter's mother.

"How are you, Louise?" she asked, as I walked to a chair near her desk and sat down.

"Fine. Thank you so much for seeing me again," I said, feeling very fragile.

"What is so important to me is that you saw and talked with my daughter's mother. It's overwhelmingly appealing to just look at you knowing that." I blurted this out and immediately wondered if I'd said more than I should.

"I was truly amazed that they still live in the same house as they did sixteen years ago." Barbara sounded professional and distant.

"Yes, that family's stability is wonderful. Knowing that has calmed a mass of guilt." My eyes filled with tears.

"What does my daughter's mother look like?" The thin veneer of calmness I possessed peeled away with this question.

"She is very different from you." Barbara said. "I can't tell you more."

"Can you tell me my daughter's first name?" Once again trapped in my maze, I bounced off the walls with this question.

"No, I cannot. The confines of the law do not allow me to give you any information of this sort. I did see a picture of your daughter. She is very pretty, with dark eyes and long dark hair."

Hearing that sent me back to the past, where a dimpled baby with large eyes momentarily flashed in my mind.

I knew the next question was forbidden, but I heard myself ask, "Can you tell me where she lives?"

"I can only say she lives a long way from you." Barbara looked understandably uncomfortable.

"Your daughter's mother was somewhat wary of your peripheral presence but brave enough to drive here to get your health history." There was anger in her voice. Or was it my own fear that I felt?

I wanted to be appropriate, and yet my mind remembered my juvenile plan to scan every high school yearbook in the city where she lived in hopes of recognizing her. My eyes filled with tears as my naive intention dimmed with the reality of finding out so little.

"I'm sorry, but this is all I can share." Barbara's words had a note of finality.

I struggled to appear comfortable, or at least grateful, that my health history had been passed along, but instead I felt overwhelmed at having come to a dead end. At no time since I had leaped from my closet of silence did I experience such a thud of despair.

My heaviness was softened when Barbara said, "I want you to know that meeting you has given me a different point of view when talking to unwed mothers."

"Thank you for all you've done. I know it's all you can do." I left Barbara's office with all of its secrets intact.

When I got into my car I felt like the bottom had fallen out from under me. Beyond the yearbook idea—which necessitated knowing the city where my daughter lived—I did not know where to go or how to proceed. The agency information lit a tiny candle in the dark room I had entered, but now I was driven by my momentum to acquire more information. I developed an instant, frantic impatience. I wanted the entire room lit, yet I was still in the dark.

Like a visibly deflated balloon, my wails of grief accompanied me home. A layer of discouragement coated my determination to someday meet my daughter. Without that hope my future seemed like sand running through my fingers. My husband Paul was tired of my tears, and even the CUB women could not console me. My friends suggested I see a therapist.

There was a low-cost clinic in the city where I lived. I called and made an appointment. I was assigned to a young female intern whom I saw three times. At our first session I unravelled the past and explained the problem I was experiencing with depression at having seemingly lost the thread leading to my daughter.

"I could have the doctor here prescribe some antidepressants," she said calmly.

"I don't want to camouflage my symptoms," I said, uncharacteristically assertive, "I want to find my daughter." I began crying. She handed me some tissues.

"It sounds like you need to stop your search. It seems to be causing you such distress," she said, patting my hand.

"I want to learn how to cope with my sadness, my sense of hopelessness. I don't want to stop searching," I replied.

"All adoption files are confidential. They are sealed. There is no way that you will get the information you seek. Look at where your efforts have taken you." Her voice had a positive edge of authority.

"I've come a long way. I can't stop now." I began crying again. She handed me more tissues.

Our first hour together was a tug-of-war. I pulled for the right to keep searching, and she to help me see that my search would only lead to more depression.

At our second meeting, I characteristically relinquished my power. This time, I endeavored to swallow as my own all of her negativity regarding searching for my daughter. I left with a knot in my stomach—more depressed than ever.

I amazed myself during our third session when I unleashed my will and shared that I was moved to continue my search, no matter what difficulty lay ahead. She blew up.

"I think you should permanently drop the whole idea." She looked deadly serious as she spoke. "You gave your daughter to adoption sixteen years ago. You made your decision then."

"But I was not prepared for all the regret and guilt I'm facing now," I spoke politely retreating into deeply ingrained respect.

"You are doing a great disservice to the people who adopted your daughter. I fear that if you were ever to meet your daughter, she'd be as disturbed as you are and end up in therapy herself. What you are doing is morally wrong." She shouted the last two words as if to emphasize her tirade.

I was unprepared for her outburst. My voice left me. Tears disintegrated into sobs. All of the ALMA sessions, all of the research validating reunions as positive, faded at that moment. I again became the weak, insecure child, ashamed because she had been bad.

"I need to leave," I said—and yet felt tied to my chair.

"Everything you're doing is hurting your daughter, and you are being self-destructive."

"I need to leave," I whispered through my tears. This time my nerve showed up from some unexpected source and guided me out the door.

Alone at home I wondered if she was right. Was I hurting myself? Would I disrupt my daughter's life if I were to meet her? I was deadly afraid of seeing the therapist again.

The next day I called and cancelled our next appointment. Our conversation was short and unpleasant.

"This is not the way to end therapy," she angrily responded.

"I don't feel this is working out. I came to you to alleviate my guilt and our sessions have instead compounded it." I was surprised and proud of myself as I confronted her wrath.

"You are trying to demean me with your words. You must come in one more time." There was a heavy silence.

"I will not come in again." I felt fleetingly unassailable. I hung up, immediately called an ALMA member and recounted my dilemma. An adoptee himself, Brian encouraged me to honor my feelings.

"You ought not be terrified of your therapist," he said. "A woman in her position should not judge, no matter what her belief on the issue is. She is very typical of the archaic lack of understanding surrounding adoption."

"Thanks for your help on the matter. It's so easy to doubt myself," I said softly.

"I know. All of us in the triangle have been judged when we step out of the mold of blind acceptance. Will you be at the next ALMA meeting?"

"Yes, I'll see you there." The call was short and temporarily helpful.

I dragged a heavy burden into the next ALMA meeting. It was vividly clear that the roots of my fear and doubt were deep. Receiving support from adoptees and birthparents was comforting, but a small voice within me wondered if I was only a dreamer—perhaps I would never find my daughter.

Doubts not withstanding, I never returned for any more therapy sessions. That act demanded a huge measure of self-confidence and required that I touch base with some of my anger as well. It was years before I saw another therapist.

I continued with CUB meetings, and my weekly public service announcements unearthed new birthmothers each month. During those days I often felt I was floating just above my discouragement. My thoughts were persistently bound to Barbara. Dreams became magnets pulling me back to The Infant of Prague Agency. This woman was the closest link I had to my daughter's identity. She was the keeper of the pot of gold, and I was moved to write her once more.

Dear Barbara,

When I last visited you I wrestled with many discordant feelings knowing you had talked to my daughter's mother.

Information gained through you has given me a clearer vision of past fantasy. Knowing that my child, now a young woman, is in a loving, stable home relieves many morbid, illusory fears. Knowing she has dark eyes and long dark hair is precious truth, but I want more. I want to see her—I want to meet her face-to-face.

I remember your parting words about having a different point of view when talking to pregnant unwed mothers since you've met me. Hopefully, you can incorporate the challenge I've faced and offer a more realistic support system to others who, for whatever reason, surrender their children to adoption.

There is a deep jealousy that I confront these days. It seems I gave up such a jewel, and though I am aware that jewels are not just born but are nurtured and guided, I am paradoxically grateful to her adoptive family as well as envious.

Though this knowledge gained through your help is bitter-sweet, it is preferable to knowing nothing. I suspect I have threatened this family with my emergence, however distant, in their lives.

If it is appropriate you might send them my thanks. They can relax.
I do not want to steal "their daughter." You are a warm person, and
I thank you for your help.

> *Sincerely,*
> *Louise Jurgens*

I did not hear from Barbara. My surest protection was to maintain contact with CUB, although it was becoming clear that for many there was little emotional booty to be gained in the search. I now see us as victims in a drama, contributing and sharing occasional victories. Most of the members had birthchildren who were under eighteen, and ALMA search workshops were not open to them. Those whose birthchildren were older often faced enormous obstacles when they probed the past. Bureaucratic resistance was phenomenal. Leads, more often than not, became detours which in turn became endless circles. We resembled a troop of worn-out crusaders. Laws existed behind locked doors aching to be flung open, with their darkened rooms waiting to be searched.

Sporadic reunions were celebrated, and each event sparked life back into us. We wanted proof that children surrendered to adoption did not hate their birthparents. We wanted proof that it was possible to develop a friendship with our children, and though each reunion was unique, not once were we disappointed. Wounds began to heal when contact was made.

At about that time, I learned that documents signed before relinquishment were legally accessible.

Barbara was the logical recipient of my "newfound rights." It was inconceivable that I had not been told of my rights sixteen years before. The vague contempt I had for the agency was building to full scale anger. I felt manipulated. Who best to hear my concerns but Barbara? I wrote her again.

Dear Barbara,

Since I last wrote to you it has come to my attention that I have a legal right to all files and documents pertaining to me and my daughter prior to the date that I signed relinquishment papers. I have the right to her original certificate of birth, the surrender warrant, the adoption decree, the notes taken by the social worker, medical consent papers and hospital and financial records. (I used my college savings and the fifty dollar monthly stipend earned at the wage home to pay all costs at the maternity hospital.) Since the information above is what was asked of or obtained from me, and does not in any way divulge secrecy, there is no logical or legal reason I cannot have a copy of them.

I wrote for and received my daughter's baptismal certificate. Of course it contains nothing I didn't already know, since it was I who named her. But having this piece of paper somehow helps. Can you send me copies of the above papers? I am told they are in my daughter's file.

Also, when last in your office I was afraid to ask outright what my daughter looked like. Can you remember anything in addition to her dark eyes and hair? I know you only saw a picture, but any comment about what you remember would be appreciated. Can you tell me what her mother looks like? I have a fantasy of her looking like Sada Thompson, the actress on the TV series "Family." I have dreams about her and we always hug. Can knowing that she is tall or short, thin or plump, blonde or dark-haired be divulging so much? I anxiously await your response.

Sincerely,
Louise Jurgens

I did not hear from Barbara. She had already communicated that bureaucracy made further intervention impossible for her. She never sent me the papers I asked for, and I never pursued my request because I was sidetracked.

My relationship with my husband was becoming very shaky. It became obvious that our relationship worked fine if I was stable, optimistic and confident. But the adoption issue had stretched my strength tissue-thin. Paul was not emotionally equipped to deal with my inner conflicts. Although he was giving all he could, the complexities of my guilt exceeded the degree of intimacy our relationship had fostered. We became strangers living in the same house. I had to look to myself for meaning, and most of the time my meager skills felt grossly inadequate to cope with my struggle.

Some joys and strengths did surface during those days. The day Von Wilmont called was special. He was the host of a popular, local radio show whose phone-in format excited me. I was representing CUB and hopeful that I could expand individuals' perceptions concerning the sensitive issue of adoptees meeting birthparents.

The following is a short excerpt from that interview. It represents the tightly held opinions and fears common in the late seventies. That human nature is fragile was reflected in the views shared that morning. So often the human need to be right destroys potential for growth and movement. But the hope of opening a few minds that day was a welcome challenge.

As I listened to the tape in order to extract the heart of its content, I was carried into nostalgia.

Von Wilmont: We're talking about adoption with Louise Jurgens from Concerned United Birthparents, an organization of parents who gave up their children, or "surrendered" as Louise says.

Caller: I just tuned into the program. It's fascinating and sounds like a very worthwhile group. I'm an adopted adult and I think what you're doing is great. If my mother had joined an organization like yours and found me, I'd have been delighted.

That first call settled me into the illusion of false comfort. The next one jarred me into reality.

VON WILMONT: We have another caller on the line.

CALLER: I feel the child is the victim here and don't think the birth-parents should have any rights. There would be a great deal of trauma to the adopted child were he to meet the birthparents. I know many beautifully adjusted, adopted children and they should not be contacted. It might make their lives miserable.

VON WILMONT: Thank you, let us do just that, talk about the child. Louise, what about that, are the children just victims?

LOUISE: I don't like to hear the adoptee being referred to as a child because that little infant grows up and turns into a fifty-, sixty- and seventy-year old adult. There are in ALMA some seventy-five-year-olds looking for their genealogical past. Certainly, their biological parents are not alive anymore. I would urge this lady and others who feel that reunions are damaging to read the book, *The Adoption Triangle*. The authors are pioneers in this field. The stereotype of the scared teenage girl and boy surrendering their child to adoption is archaic. The birthparents also mature and become thirty-, forty- and fifty-year-olds. Research proves that when there are meetings, it resolves pain, and it does not matter who initiates the search. What occurs is a resolution of guilt, frustration and anxiety, and it is generally not traumatic.

CALLER: I'm an adoptive parent of two children and I want to stress that there is a lot of pain adopting children. I don't think birth-parents should have any right to seek them out. I don't want the fear of someone taking our babies back. We have given them all they need and want.

LOUISE: It would be wonderful if people in our society began to recognize that curiosity and interest in one's lineage speaks well of a healthy inquisitive mind. In any other circumstance this brings enthusiastic endorsement from everyone in the community, including the family. But, it does not seem to be accepted as of yet for an adoptee to want to meet a birthparent, or a birthparent to want to meet the child who was surrendered to adoption. When a human face replaces a fantasy, the beginning of wisdom begins to be injected into people's minds who dared to see reconciliation as good. Society needs its citizens to attune with one another and that includes the adult adoptee, the birthparents and the adoptive parents.

CALLER: My sister adopted two infant brothers who are now in their mid-twenties. About three years ago their birthfather called and wanted to know if he could have her permission to visit his sons. She was delighted. She gave him the boys' names, addresses and telephone numbers, and he went to see them. The whole visit was friendly and amiable. They love their adoptive mother no less. She gave them someone important to know, and someone else to love.

LOUISE: The heart of the matter that this caller points out is that whether we give birth to our children or adopt them, we don't own them. They are given to us for a few years to raise, and if we love them wisely and do our jobs well, we may hope to merit their love and esteem. Adoptive parents occasionally try to bring up adopted children without telling them the truth about their origin. There is the strong possibility that this lie will collapse like a house of cards. We need to realize that parenthood is not biological.

VON WILMONT: We're talking to Louise Jurgens, one of thousands of women who has surrendered a child to adoption.

Calls continued all morning. As each person shared viewpoints, what surfaced was the unending search for personal validation. It looked as if much of humanity was tightly wrapped in a cocoon, and no matter how uncomfortable they felt, most were hesitant to break through.

7

The Miracle

No sense wishing for a past we can't do anything about.
Why not wish for things we still can do!
—RICHARD BACH

The main gift hidden in that radio broadcast was that it led to a call from a reporter from *The Sacramento Bee*. He had heard the interview and asked if I would come in and speak with him. My expectations were minimal. I thought this meeting would result in a short public service paragraph concerning CUB. Much to my surprise, the reporter spoke with me for over an hour. He took reams of notes, asked about me personally and requested that I wait to get photographed.

Not long afterwards, an article appeared in the local newspaper. It was a full page and included a picture. I was delightfully stunned. Titled "My Daughter Is Alive and Well," the write-up detailed my life and search. My address and phone number were incorporated into the piece with this quote ending the feature:

I've been told to grieve for my daughter as if she were dead and get it over with, but that is impossible. She's not dead, and I refuse to stop hoping that we'll meet.

The article elicited enormous response, all of it favorable. I received calls from policemen, teachers, adoptees and birthmothers, all of whom were encouraging and reassuring. One teacher said she'd look at birthdates of students and call me back if one matched.

Unbelievably, I was recognized on downtown streets and applauded for my courage. My years of hiding seemed foolish indeed. During all of my media exposure, I never once received negative input. This positive support unearthed the shallow masquerade of thinking that I did not have a deep need for acceptance.

Up to this time I had felt like a traitor to my family, but now, with strangers accepting me, I unearthed a desire to have my parents support me as well. I had only guardedly shared my search with them, and they were not overly enthusiastic. Their understanding was stuck in a belief system that did not embrace adoption reunions. I had only recently burst the bubble of secrecy with my brothers who, though shocked and saddened by the years of silence, rigidly believed that I was bent on a destructive course.

Wanting to include my family more intimately in my life prompted me to mail the article to them. Having never before guessed at the extent of my seriousness, each was staggered by what seemed to them an exposé. Phone calls and letters guaranteed that I was unmasking a sensitive and painful issue. My family was especially worried that I would only be hurt if I met my daughter, and that I would disrupt her life.

My best friend Michelle benevolently wrote to my brother Edward and his wife on my behalf. Receiving a copy of her letter allowed me to see how supportive she was.

> Dear Edward and Ellen,
>
> As Louise's old friend and as an adoptive parent of a son who is now ten, I hope you won't mind if I share some of my views with you. Louise has told me that you want her to give up her search.

I've worked as an adoption social worker in California and in Chicago and I've had considerable in-service training. I've talked to many natural parents and adoptees. In Chicago, I worked primarily with adoptive parents.

From all I have learned, Louise's desire to know about her daughter seems natural rather than neurotic. Everyone in the "adoption triangle" wonders about each other through the years. The extent of this wondering, and whether any action is taken, depends entirely on the individual, and can vary greatly.

Although not every child will actually look for his parents, I believe that very few would turn down the opportunity to meet them. Some adoptees have gone to unbelievable expenditures of time and money to find their birthmothers.

Despite all the unknowns in this situation, I believe Louise knows what she is doing. Rather than arousing long-term anxiety for her in the future, I believe this search will probably resolve long-term anxiety from the past.

Louise's interest in this is nothing new. I do hope you will give this some thought.

> *Sincerely,*
> *Michelle*

Michelle's letter fell on deaf ears. But, I was intoxicated with pursuing my vision of someday meeting my daughter, and blind to my family's reticence. They were wrapped in layers of judgement and dogma, and entangled in society's mores and rigid rules. How could they release the tight grip that fear had threaded in their lives? Masters at being out of touch with their own feelings, how could they understand mine?

Two days after *The Sacramento Bee* article, I received a call from the purveyor of my miracle. It was an undeniable gift from a higher source. At four o'clock in the afternoon the phone rang, and a voice on the line commented on having read my story.

"I was moved by it and want to help," the speaker said.

"How can you help?" I was more puzzled than curious.

"If I could, I would tell you your daughter's name and where she lives."

"Who are you?" I asked, this time more than curious.

"I can't tell you that. I can only say I've long worked in adoptions and have seen some horror stories over the years." I instinctively reached for a sheet of paper.

"I have access to a skeleton file, and I have your daughter's parents' names. I feel sharing this with you, helping you in this small way, might make up for other's misfortunes."

"Their names?" I heard the words through a filter of disbelief.

"They are Thomas Brian White and Rosetta Mae White." The caller spelled the names as I wrote them down.

I wept softly, staring at the slip of paper with the names of my daughter's parents.

"You have given me a key to unlock a precious secret. Thanks is a hollow word that scarcely touches my joy, but it's all that comes to mind." I wept again with my hand firmly clutching the sheet of paper with the two names, my quintessential prize.

I asked how many years the caller had worked in adoptions. There was no answer to my question. The entire phone conversation took less than two minutes. I whispered my thanks again and then heard the sound of a dial tone.

Staring at the names gave substance to my phantom amputation. Recalling my daughter's birth, I was instantly transplanted into the past with the name White. Nothing, before or since, has matched the catharsis I experienced that afternoon.

Sitting in the warm sunlit room, I sobbed endlessly, tears flowing like a chanted litany that drained me on the one hand and also strengthened my resolve. I marvelled at the inexhaustible humor of a French-Italian, German-Filipino named White.

The name conjured up a phone directory nightmare equal to finding a Smith, Davis or Brown. I hoped there were not too many

White's with the first name of Thomas, and I prayed that my White's were listed.

That same week Paul and I decided to divorce, and he moved out. I felt ambivalent, being both elated with my discovery and disheartened about the divorce. The pain was eased by the surge of hope that had been rekindled after my miraculous phone call.

Alone once again, I shared my treasure with friends and ALMA and CUB members. The days following Paul's departure were spent looking through hundreds of phone books and nervously calling each Thomas White. None were married to a Rosetta Mae.

Deeper than my frustration was a tenacity that magnetized me to the task. The universe was on my wavelength, as once again an extraordinary phone call pushed open another door.

"Hello, is this Louise Jurgens?" An unfamiliar voice queried me. "Yes, this is Louise."

"I'm a friend of a friend of yours, Sherry Parks. She's an adoptee who's been searching for her birthmother."

"Yes, I know Sherry through ALMA."

"She told me about the name you have, and your phone directory search."

"Yes, White is a rather common name, and I've had little luck."

"I think I can help you."

"How?" My curiosity peaked.

"This may sound a bit strange, but I know a technique that is very powerful."

"What?" I asked impatiently.

"It's rather esoteric. It involves a pendulum. Were I to hang one over a California map it would tell me where your daughter lives. Are you interested?" he asked.

"Yes, I am." The procedure sounded potentially harmless. We arranged to meet at my house the next evening.

He arrived exactly on time, and after a microsecond dealing with introductions and social pleasantries, he unfolded a large, California road map on the living room floor.

He took out a ring attached to a short, gold chain. He held this pendulum, as he called it, over each city on the map starting with Los Angeles. I watched the pendulum slowly inch northward. It swung sideways at each stop.

All of my attention was as focused on this object as a cat watching a fly on the wall. When the pendulum reached Bakersfield it suddenly changed its direction and began spinning clockwise. I struggled to understand why this intense, quiet man suddenly looked so happy.

"If it spins clockwise, that's a yes," he said answering my thoughts.

"She lives in Bakersfield?" I asked. Though the reality of forces beyond my comprehension had long been a fascination, I strained to believe this was true.

"I have no doubt that you'll find the Whites you're looking for in that city," he said, neatly folding up his map.

"I will certainly check it out tomorrow," I said.

His job done, this emissary of light picked up his folded map and left.

The following day, I jumped into my car and drove directly to the state library. I went upstairs and looked for Thomas Brian White in the 1961 Bakersfield directory. There he was! Seconds later, I found the same listing in the current Bakersfield directory. Luxuriating in the glow of hope and joy, I was humbled by the effectiveness of a man's pendulum swinging clockwise over a spot on a map.

No dream about my daughter had ever contained such concreteness. With a firm grip on yet another slip of paper representing my grandest prize to date, I studied another book to learn more about the people who were my daughter's parents. This was the *Polk Directory*. It crisscrosses facts. You can check an address to find out who lives there, obtain names of spouses, and also find out information about a person's job. There I read that Thomas Brian White worked for an established utilities company.

As I left the library and headed for my car I felt like an iceberg, calm and insignificant on the surface and yet intensely potent. But this sense of strength soon evaporated as my exhilaration blinded me to the location of my car. After searching with mounting frustration, I stopped at a downtown office to get help. I knew Betty worked there. It seemed fitting that I share my news with her first, for she was the first adoptee I had met. She spotted my car instantly. I had passed it four times.

"I wish I could have your luck," she said, hugging me.

"You haven't found your birthmother yet?" I had heard she was close.

"I always think the next clue will be it, but it hasn't happened. You've been so lucky."

"I'm aware of that." I felt compassion for Betty. I had just begun my search, while she had been looking for ten years.

"What will you do now?" she asked.

"I'm not sure. I'll let you know."

Back home at my desk, I sat reflecting on my next move.

Wanting to absolutely validate the accuracy of the *Polk Directory*, I decided to call the number. Too shaky to trust my ability to ad-lib, I wrote a script and practiced it a few times.

Picking up the phone, I dialed the number. A girl answered. It was a young voice.

"Is this Rosetta Mae White's residence?" I read.

"Yes it is," the girl answered.

"The Salvation Army will be in your neighborhood next week. Does your family have any clothing or furniture to donate at this time?" My mind wondered at my awkward approach.

"I don't know. My mother is in Fresno. She won't be home for a few days."

"We'll call back next week." Then, unable to contain my curiosity, I asked, "To whom am I speaking?"

"This is Tammy."

"Thank you. We'll call when your mom returns." I was no longer reading my script. My hand shook as I gently cradled the phone.

"Tammy," I said out loud. Could this be my daughter? I assumed I had just spoken to my daughter, and that her name was Tammy.

I knew *The Sacramento Bee* had a parent paper in Fresno so I called the editor and told him about the incredible events of the preceding days, and asked if he could wire my story to Fresno. He was delighted to do so.

Was it pure chance that my daughter's mother was in Fresno at this moment in time? Was there a supernatural design that *The Sacramento Bee* have a parent paper in that same city? Was I fashioning my miracle when I called the editor? Something was preordained because there was no resistance. This time, fate was smiling on me.

Basking in the miraculous gave energy to my vision. I firmly believed that my daughter's mother would spot the article, recognize me as her daughter's birthmother and call.

Two days later, on a Sunday evening, I answered the phone, that messenger of good fortune, and an operator asked, "Will you accept a call from your daughter's mother?"

Weakly, I answered, "Yes." My knuckles turned white as I gripped the phone, fearing that it would fly away. Her first words were a question.

"Will this article appear anywhere else?" There was fear in her voice.

"I don't believe so," I answered.

"I saw the headline, 'Hello Miss Fresnan, Are You the Baby They Made Me Give Away?' and was very surprised at what I read."

"That was not the headline here in Sacramento," I responded, feeling apologetic for the soap opera change made in the story title.

"What is it that you want?"

I felt this to be a fair and honest question.

"I have no desire to disrupt your life or my birthdaughter's. I realize she is, at this time, only sixteen," I answered, grabbing paper and a pen.

I doubt that my memory would have drawn a blank at this moment, but I wrote down every word shared in this call.

"I would like to ask that my birthdaughter be allowed to know my identity sometime after she reaches eighteen, if you are comfortable with that."

There was no immediate answer, and then I heard, "Your daughter . . . my daughter was told she was adopted when she was very young. She has not spoken about her adoptive status recently." The voice was calm, and yet I sensed a wariness.

Again, neither of us spoke. I marvelled that I was talking to my daughter's mother, knowing instinctively that nothing would be gained by revealing my knowledge of her identity. It was my time to guard a secret.

Mrs. White continued, "Her middle name, interestingly, is the same name you gave her, Marie."

I ached to ask what her first name was, but I knew that was sacred ground. Swallowing my question, I felt the orchestration of this part of my miracle was in divine hands and needed nothing from me but my presence. Mingled with my own thoughts, my daughter's mother shared another gift with her next words.

"Since you're a schoolteacher I assume you might be interested in knowing that her IQ is 136."

My grip on the phone loosened as I listened.

"Her weakest subject is math."

"I wonder if that could be genetic," I revealed. "My weakest subject was also math."

Seeming more comfortable with sharing, Mrs. White continued,

"She had to have orthodontia for her teeth when she was younger. The dentist's observation was that perhaps her quarter Filipino ancestry created a smaller bone structure than was needed."

I wrote as Mrs. White generously shared more about my daughter. Each anecdote stripped away a layer from the past.

"She began menstruating at eleven."

"Perhaps that is also hereditary. I began my periods at ten."

There was a momentary pause, and then anxiety filled the gentle voice on the phone.

"I was concerned about the cancer that was mentioned in the newspaper article and in the health history I picked up at The Infant of Prague Adoption Agency."

"It is, unfortunately, a fact on my mother's side of the family. On my father's side there seems to be a penchant for heart attacks."

Since we were sharing in this vein I allowed myself to speak about my endometriosis, explaining the details of my surgery as Mrs. White listened quietly.

"Your daughter . . . my daughter has not had any problems of that sort," Mrs. White assured me.

Again, there was a slight pause. Then my daughter's mother continued sharing.

"We are Catholic converts and always wanted a large family. Your daughter attends a Catholic high school and has been raised as a Catholic."

A stream of light from the window reflected off my pen as I wrote, indelibly etching a word-picture of my child. I noticed that the fear in Mrs. White's voice had disappeared. She spoke with a simplicity and clarity; her willingness was my treasure.

"My daughter . . . your daughter, has long dark hair and can almost sit on it. It is very thick and often braided."

As she spoke I remembered the picture in my wallet of a ten-year-old Louise with ankle-length dark, thick hair. It was the very picture on which I chose to write my daughter's birthdate, name and weight as I cried in an empty church sixteen years before.

It was my turn to share. "I never cut my hair until I was in my early teens. It was also thick and long and worn in braids." I struggled to hide my tears. I was in uncharted territory, and my mind told me to camouflage the tears which felt like inappropriate enemies. I wanted nothing to frighten my precious caller away.

"When she was young, she said she wanted to be an Indian. Not cutting her hair was part of that parcel. She felt that if she looked like an Indian, she would get a horse. We bought her a horse when she was six, and she began taking riding lessons." Her voice flowed with love. As she spoke I saw my daughter as a fanciful, strong-willed child, and this mental sketch eased me into a smile.

"From the picture in the newspaper article she has your eyes. She is five-feet-three and very athletic," Mrs. White continued.

A multiple presence magnetized around me as I listened. A treasured gift was before me—the parent-mother and the birthmother touching for the first time. I wanted to applaud Mrs. White's courage in calling, but my own shyness and sense of awe did not allow me to deviate from the rigidity of listening and writing.

"I'm five-feet-two," I finally said.

"The article mentioned musical interests. She does not sing but is an excellent pianist."

I continued to create images of my daughter as Mrs. White's words filled the distance between us. The notes from this first conversation became the proverbial bronzed shoe. I have saved them to this day.

"She has an excellent hourglass figure," my daughter's mother added.

As I wrote, an unspoken "thank you" hugged each word on my notepaper, and yet my deepest questions and humblest gratitude were buried deep within.

"She drives and has a part-time job. She has always been persistently determined to conquer all things and has been an independent individual all her life."

I silently wondered if that was genetic. My own determination has often been at odds with my fears, yet I have always been persistent.

"When she was four, she wanted to ride a two-wheeled bike. She wanted to learn alone and mastered it in three days after many falls."

My admiration for my daughter's mother crystallized at this point, and I finally mustered the courage to whisper through stifled tears, "Thank you for sharing all of this with me."

There was silence. Then Mrs. White replied, "These days she is spending less time with her horse because she has discovered dating. I have two other daughters and a son, all older than your daughter. They have a strong love for her. She is very mature for her age."

Again there was a momentary silence, and then I heard what I did not want to know.

"She has not expressed any curiosity about meeting you. I will share what I know about you if she asks when she gets older."

"I have no desire to intrude in your life or that of my birth-daughter's. I only wish to meet her someday and, if possible, to be her friend," I said, hoping my intentions did not offend or frighten her.

The silence that followed lasted only seconds, but this pause signaled the end of our conversation. After a quick good-bye, I was returned to the present by the sound of the dial tone. I reread my notes countless times, watching each anecdote transform the baby I had lost into a young woman. Knowing that my daughter was healthy and happy was an opiate of peace. For the first time the pictures I had created were more than fantasy.

Filled with optimism and joy, I called my parents later that week to share about the phone call. I hoped it would loosen some of their fears. They were unmoved and tenaciously refused to support my continued desire to someday meet my daughter.

"Louise," my dad pleaded, "you know she's okay. Now leave it alone. What if she doesn't want to meet you? We don't want you to be hurt."

"Whatever happens, it's my pain. There have been too many doors opened for me to look the other way."

"Hardheaded, stubborn, that's what you are."

"We just want you to be safe." My mother's voice was soft.

"I know you care, that you want what is best for me, but my course cannot be changed."

I heard them sigh in unison as we said our good-byes. Though my search in and of itself represented a rebellion against my parents, I nevertheless still had an intense need for their approval. Wanting to ease their apprehension, and knowing their resistance was born out of misguided concern, I shaped my thoughts into a letter.

Dear Mom and Dad,

I don't know where to start after our talk on the phone. There is so much I want to share. It is difficult to explain how I feel since I spoke to my daughter's mother.

I've been buried in guilt ever since her birth and relinquishment, never able to talk to you until now because I feared reopening old wounds, sensing that you also felt sadness over the inevitable decisions made in the past. Finding my daughter has injected light where none existed before.

I know you are worried because you love me. I know you fear more pain for me if I meet her, but I know there is a divine wisdom guiding me, and that connection has sparked all of the miracles that have been so lavishly gifted.

I learned so many wonderful things about her. My only goal is to protect and not hurt her, and I have a profound certainty that I will meet her in the future.

I hope this letter helps soothe your fears. It is certainly not all-inclusive, as that would require a book.

I love you both,
Louise

My parents remained cautious, while my detective instincts were wetted with the knowledge that my daughter attended a Catholic high school in Bakersfield. The following year my daughter would graduate. I formulated a plan to purchase a yearbook, so that I could have a photograph and learn her first name.

Years before, when I taught and lived one hour east of Sacramento in Placerville, I had become close friends with a student teacher, Martha Cooper, who was assigned to my classes. We never lost contact and remembering she was a Catholic, born and raised in Bakersfield, prompted me to call her for help. I knew she would be supportive, as she had closely and positively followed my search.

"Yes, Louise," she said, "there is only one Catholic high school. It's Garces. I attended there."

After a brief update on the search and my conversation with Mrs. White, we decided it was best if she wrote for the yearbook using her name and address. For all I knew, my daughter's mother may have worked there. It was not my intention to cause any apprehension in the White family. I didn't want them to fear me.

Though that year was uneventful, I never lost sight of my vision. I continued with my CUB activities while my parents rested securely in the belief that I had let go of ever meeting my daughter. I never again spoke to them of my undying goal. Divinely patient, my sight was fixed on graduation day. I often fantasized attending the ceremony and secretly watching my daughter receive her diploma.

Martha called the day she received the yearbook. Her enthusiasm matched mine.

I asked, "What does she look like?"

"She's very pretty and has long dark hair and dark eyes," Martha answered.

"I'm on my way. See you in one hour." I drove as if I were piloting toward heaven.

Arriving at my friend's house, I half expected to see a magical star lighting the sky. After a round of hugs and greetings, I was led to the kitchen. There on the table lay the yearbook.

"I'll let you find her. You've been on target so far on your own," Martha said.

As I thumbed nervously through the yearbook, my breathing stopped the instant my eyes spotted White. Peripheral vision simultaneously sighted her name and face in the same microsecond. The

name "Rosanne White" was beautifully written in calligraphy. With my eyes glued on her bright smile, the old fantasies dissolved like shadows in the light, replaced with the clarity of the truth before me.

She was indeed beautiful, and her name was Rosanne. After seventeen years my daughter finally had a name. Of the thousands I had imagined, "Rosanne" had never surfaced. Her dimples inexplicably proved she was mine, or perhaps it was her long dark hair and radiant eyes.

With a slow methodical hand, I looked at each page in the yearbook, spotting her in various group pictures. Paradoxically, my joy was mingled with the contradiction of sadness as each picture unearthed regret.

"Pretty amazing," I said, looking at Martha who sat beside me.

"Yes, it is a miracle, as you keep saying."

"I'd love to have an eight by ten enlargement of this picture," I sighed.

"That might be easy."

"Do you know the Bakersfield studio who takes the yearbook photos?" I asked with mounting interest.

"I can find out. My parents still live in Bakersfield, and they would probably know."

Soon after and with Martha's help, I found the studio which had taken the yearbook pictures, and when Martha went to visit her parents that same month, she ordered an enlargement, armed with a story about grandparents requesting a copy.

When I received the photo, I framed it and placed it on the wall in my bedroom. It has been there ever since. Though tempted to frame the fifteen dollar check written to purchase the yearbook, I was content with putting it in a safe place along with all my other treasures.

The intensity of my longing for a link to this child began to subside when I saw her in the photograph. But with this prize I unmasked a bitterness that stemmed from wondering what might have been. I was a walking definition of an enigmatic paradox. My joy at knowing my daughter's identity was as thrilling as any I had ever known. Yet other memories propelled me backwards in time to the darkest places where sadness lived. As I looked at her picture each day, I never ceased being staggered by the miracle. But despite the joy, I cried with regret.

8

Through the Maze

It is only with the heart that one can see rightly; what is essential is invisible to the eye.
—ANTOINE DE SAINT-EXUPÉRY

A year after I discovered where my daughter lived, I drove to Southern California to visit my parents. My musician friend Mark decided to car pool with me, as he had a music engagement for the weekend in Los Angeles that was only two hours north of where my parents lived.

When we reached Bakersfield Mark blurted out, "Why don't we drive past your daughter's home?"

"What? Oh, my God, I've had that fantasy hundreds of times but I'd be too scared to really do it. They might see me and recognize me from the newspaper pictures." Though I protested, my heart rejoiced at the idea.

We don't have to drive up and honk or anything," Mark continued, "just sneak a drive past the house. You do have the address memorized, I assume?" Mark laughed.

"Yes, you nut, and I also just happen to have a Bakersfield map in the car." The idea looked overwhelmingly attractive. "Well, maybe we could drive past and I could slouch down." I looked at Mark. He was wearing a big, funky hat.

"Give me your hat."

"What?"

"Give me your hat. My disguise—you know—it'll make me less recognizable," I said, grabbing his hat and plopping it on my head.

"You look like a stranger to me," Mark laughed again.

"Okay, you do the navigating. I'll drive."

Mark quickly pulled out the Bakersfield map, not at all amazed that I had memorized the address. The street was easy to locate.

"When we get close, I want you to drive so I can focus my attention on looking."

"You got it." Mark seemed excited about the detective-like scenario.

Soon enough, when we were only blocks from the house, Mark took the driver's seat.

"You okay?" Mark asked, noticing me stiffen and slump down in the seat.

"Yes, I just don't want to be noticed."

"Relax. We'll drive by looking really ordinary. No one will be the wiser."

A few minutes later I spotted the house.

I wanted to stop and stare at it, but instead I whispered, "Slow down a little."

"Oh, now she wants me to slow down. And you don't have to whisper. No one will hear us."

"I know, I just can't help it. My God, Mark, it's so perfect. Can you believe it? This is my daughter's home. This is where she grew up." My eyes were fixed on the house, memorizing every detail. When we reached the corner Mark asked, "I don't suppose you'd like to go past one more time?"

"Yes. Did you notice the nursery across the street?"

"I did. Want to drive in there and stop for a minute?"

"You're reading my mind."

"I know."

We did just that. Mark parked next to an old palm tree. We both got out and ran behind its giant trunk. For a moment, I forgot the clandestine atmosphere and my vague fear of being caught, as I slowly absorbed each feature. I loved the pickup, the camper and the rose bushes. It was a wonderful place.

"Isn't it a beautiful, perfect house?" I whispered.

"It's a great looking place," Mark whispered back. "Good grief, you've got me whispering, too!"

We were both watching the house, when suddenly the front door opened. A tall, thin man walked out hand-in-hand with a three- or four-year-old boy. They left in the pickup. Mark and I stayed only a few minutes more, and then we quickly jumped into the car and continued our drive to Southern California.

A few miles down the road, Mark asked, "Are you okay?"

"Yes, I'm glad I did it. I just saw my daughter's house!" I screamed. "She's had a good life. She's really fine. It's such a lovely home. Do you think anyone saw us?" I was on fast forward.

"Relax. Take a deep breath," Mark urged. "It's all going to be fine. No one knows this car, no one saw us."

We drove for a while in silence and then Mark said, "I'd be an emotional wreck, too."

"Yeah, you probably would," I said laughing.

Once in Los Angeles, Mark proceeded on to his job, and I drove to Orange County where my parents lived. Understandably, I did not feel comfortable sharing my surreptitious drive past my daughter's house. Though my family was peripherally happy that I knew her name and that she was fine, the continued, unspoken message was that I should leave well enough alone and stay out of her life. However, for me, life was centered on thoughts of someday getting a call from my daughter. That was the way I orchestrated my dream, and there was no place for static or interference in that vision.

Equally real at that time was the legal dissolution of my marriage to Paul. Were I who I am now, perhaps we would not have divorced. But neither of us had the ability to verbalize what we needed in the relationship, and disunion seemed the only way out of another long, dark tunnel.

The year following my divorce, I began teaching in Lodi, a town in central California. Though only forty-five miles south of Sacramento, the state capital, I worried that my new location might delay contact from my daughter or her mother. The newspaper article had listed what was now an old address and phone number, and since my daughter was almost nineteen, I wanted to be easily accessible. My unshakable faith that I would receive a call from Rosanne seemed only a breath away.

I communicated my concern with CUB members and received support that a push in the form of a letter might be appropriate, primarily because my daughter would soon be nineteen. This was a big step, so I conferred with several ALMA friends, who also encouraged me to write. After careful deliberation, I mailed this letter.

> *Dear Mr. and Mrs. White,*
>
> *This note might cause some apprehension. I hope it does not. Let me assure you that I have no desire to infringe upon your life or my birthdaughter's.*
>
> *I've known your identity since before your phone call of more than two years ago. I did not divulge that fact then, because I sensed your need to remain anonymous. I've made no attempt to contact my birthdaughter until now, and I've made no attempt to contact you. I hope this fact will assure you that I have no inclination to jump into your lives and cause any disruption.*
>
> *Through a series of wondrous miracles, I discovered your identity, and since our phone conversation, and the loving anecdotes you related to me about my birthdaughter, I've acquired enormous peace.*
>
> *It's gratifying to know that your life has been incredibly stable. This knowledge quieted all the irrational fears I harbored for years—that my birthdaughter was shuffled from foster home to foster home, or that she might even be dead.*
>
> *The purpose of this letter is to acquaint you with my recent move.*

I've enclosed three recent photos to add to the newspaper picture you have of me. I would very much enjoy photographs of you and your entire family should you care to mail some. Please do not fear that I will barge in on you uninvited. I will not. My hope is to someday meet you and call you and my birthdaughter friends. That is all.

Affectionately,
Louise Jurgens

After my signature, I included my new address and phone number, as well as the name and location of the school where I taught.

Several weeks passed and I did not hear from the Whites. Again, I contacted my CUB friends, as well as speaking with the ALMA president in San Francisco. I was encouraged to call Rosanne, or at least to write another letter to Mr. and Mrs. White. I decided to write to my daughter's parents once more before risking a call.

This time I included a copy of a book I'd found most helpful.

Dear Mr. and Mrs. White,

Once again, I have a desire to communicate. As you can readily see I've enclosed The Adoption Triangle. *This book presents a clear and unique look into the realm that affects adoptive parents, adoptees and birthparents. Perhaps you've already read it. If so, excuse the redundancy.*

One of the purposes of this letter is to acquaint you with some insights gained these past few years.

When I discovered my birthdaughter's identity, it was as if a missing part of the circle representing my life became filled with reality. Then, when you so courageously and generously called and shared those beautiful anecdotes, many questions were answered.

At any rate, these past few years have been more tranquil for me, especially in respect to my birthdaughter. There is less wondering and guessing.

I hope and assume that both of you have had a chance to grow calm with respect to my emergence into your lives, or at least the periphery of your lives. This time has given each of us an opportunity to digest information about one another: information that we exist, that we have names, lives and jobs that are as normal as most on this planet.

I do not know this for a fact, but I presume that you have not yet shared my identity with Rosanne. Please rest assured that if I have any expectations at all, it is to be, at best, a long-distance friend. Rosanne is your daughter.

Research proves that the parental bond between adoptee and adoptive parents is strengthened when the birthparent enters the picture. But, more to the point, we are all part of this triangle. Two parts have been exposed to each other and have had a period of integration, yet to my knowledge the third, most innocent party has not.

This brings me to the main purpose of my letter. I want to contact Rosanne, personally. I ask that you share the information you have about me with her so that she, too, can digest and assimilate it for a while before we meet.

I feel that a period of integration preceding a meeting would be beneficial, if not necessary. I do not want this to be a traumatic experience, and therefore I would like your help so that it is done in a nurturing and non-threatening way for her.

I would like to meet with you first, so that we can get to know one another before I contact Rosanne or she contacts me. If you would like to meet, please write or call me collect.

Sincerely,
Louise Jurgens

I'm not absolutely certain if, how or when, I would have contacted my daughter, but my uncertainty was handled by a higher source. A few weeks after I mailed my second letter, I received a call from Mrs. White. Our conversation was brief and presented me with my worst nightmare.

"I received your letters and have been hesitant to get back to you." Her voice undeniably held bad news.

"Is there something wrong?" I asked, knowing there was but asking the question, nonetheless.

"I think you don't want to hear what I have to say, but your last letter prompted me to call. I did share your identity with Rosanne, very soon after her eighteenth birthday."

Automatically, I grabbed a pen and paper as I listened with my heart in my throat.

"I was very nervous and scared myself, as I shared this information with her. My daughter Susan was at the kitchen table with us. They are very close, and I felt her presence would provide support. I told Rosanne that her mother was looking for her, and I invited her to join Susan and me at the table where I had the folder with the newspaper article, your pictures, the health history and letters. As Rosanne sat down, she said, 'You mean, Grandma?'"

I was perched on the edge of my chair while Mrs. White continued.

"I then told her that it was not her grandmother, but her mother. I showed her the folder. She immediately got up saying, 'I don't want to meet her.' She did not look at the contents of the folder and angrily left the room shouting, 'I don't want to talk about it. That lady threw me away eighteen years ago. I don't want to talk to her.' I told her I would leave the folder on the table if she wanted to see it later."

An interminable silence filled the room as I looked at the tear-soaked paper on my desk. My daughter's mother's words had validated the ultimate calamity. I was devastated.

"Rosanne will be married in a few months. She is doing fine and seems very happy."

"I appreciate your efforts on my behalf. Thank you for your courage and kindness," I finally said through stifled tears as we hung up.

My hand gripped the phone for several minutes, while I sobbed with no seeming end. All the fears of my daughter hating me for not keeping her became a reality with that one phone call. I called Barney, a close friend, to share what had just happened. He was not home, and I left a message on his answering machine. When he returned my call hours later, he said my voice sounded like death.

I hated myself with renewed vigor and cried for days, retreating into my familiar maze. The words, "She threw me away. I don't want to talk to her," echoed in my mind. I felt this was all I deserved. Even ALMA and CUB friends were unable to ease my grief. Finding myself in a state beyond being comforted, I burrowed into self-condemnation.

But, miracles were on the menu for me. Only a few months after my conversation with Mrs. White, I received another afternoon phone call. When I answered, I heard a young woman ask to speak to Louise Jurgens. In a millionth of a second, my mind computed that this voice belonged to my daughter. Yet hers was a voice I had never heard.

"This is Louise," I answered, holding my breath. There was an uncomfortably long pause, and then a nineteen-year-old dream came true with the next three words.

"This is Rosanne."

"I'm so glad to finally be talking to you," was all I could say as I held the phone, expecting it to fly away.

"I feel like the first person to ever talk to her birthmother." She sounded tense.

"It does feel somewhat like a movie script, or a soap opera." Once again, I instinctively found a pen and paper. This time I hoped the words would not be marred with tears.

"I'm going to be married in a month. It was Allen, my fiancé, who pushed me over the edge to call you."

"I'm very glad he did," I said, uttering the biggest understatement of my life.

There was silence for a moment, and I thought that it was odd to be struck dumb after nineteen years of aching to communicate.

"We'd both like to meet you. Would you like to come to our wedding next month?" she asked, while I pictured the young woman in the high school yearbook photograph.

"Yes, very much," I answered, still feeling helplessly tongue-tied and hoping my daughter did not think me a jerk. "We'd like to get together with you before the wedding, just to meet. Would that be okay?"

"Yes, that would be fantastic!"

"Lodi isn't too far from Bakersfield. Allen and I could come there." She sounded more relaxed with each mention of her fiancé.

"I'd love to have you both come here." I gave her directions to my house, and a specific day and time was arranged for the following week.

"I'll mail you a wedding invitation. Well, take care. We'll see you next week."

"Great, I'll see you then." For just a second we sounded like regular pals.

She hung up after final good-byes, but as I put the receiver down, my hands shook and my eyes filled with tears. Deep inside, I knew I had just touched my lost child, and I sensed that we were not pals quite yet.

We had talked for only a few minutes, but the call left me exhausted. I sat at my desk, doing nothing and aware only of my breathing.

Then, as my cat jumped on my lap, I whispered, "She called me!"

Suddenly those three words launched explosive weeping. I saw the baby I had never held, and that picture gave way to inconsolable mourning. Still crying, I pulled a card from my desk and wrote:

> *I care. I always have.*
> *Thank you for calling.*
> *Your birthmother,*
> *Louise Jurgens*

I addressed the envelope to Rosanne White, reflecting on the utter privilege of knowing her name and address and having just talked with her. But there was also a heaviness in my heart. I had just signed a note to my daughter with my full name, and I felt a chill knowing we were total strangers as I stared at it.

The notes of our first conversation lay on my desk for days. They were a cherished gift, and I never ceased being astonished at the phenomenon of actually having them in my possession. They seemed to prove that somehow, now, I would not die without first meeting my daughter.

That week I cleaned and recleaned my already clean house, tended my garden and found my life centered around that visit. I was quite literally flying. But the meeting was not to happen as scheduled. A couple of days before our planned get-together, I received another short call cancelling the visit.

"We can't make it to Lodi. Could you possibly drive to Fresno?" my daughter asked.

"Yes, of course. I'll drive to Bakersfield if that works better for you."

"No, Fresno is fine. My sister lives there, and we can meet at her place."

I wrote the directions, and a new meeting day was arranged.

There were no hitches this time. On the designated day, I was too nervous to eat. And though I felt like celebrating my joy, apprehension paralyzed me. Wondering what to wear made me feel crazy. I ended up selecting something loose-fitting and comfortable, so that at least my outer appearance would look relaxed. Dressing in neutral sandals and a lavender sun dress, I headed for Fresno. Even now, looking back on that day, I cannot decide what I should have worn.

I drove south for three hours in a state of numbness. I went alone. It was a typically hot central valley summer day, and yet I did not feel the heat.

As I drove down the street toward the house, I became aware of my racing heartbeat and my death grip on the steering wheel. I never take tranquilizers, but I wished I had some then.

Parking behind a pickup, which I assumed belonged to Allen, was easy enough, but I felt weak-kneed while walking to the house. My legs and arms were trembling as I knocked on the door. Then, seconds later, the door opened, and I was inches away from my daughter after nineteen years of separation.

I had dreamed that our first meeting would include an instant warm hug—perhaps that expectation was in her thoughts, too. But we did not touch—we just stared at one another. She looked much as I had imagined she would. Had I never seen her picture, I could have spotted her on the street.

A slight Eurasian quality punctuated her dark, expressive eyes and long dark hair. She had my eyes, mouth and body type, though her coloring was darker. The quarter Filipino, I thought.

Rosanne broke the silence.

"You're very short," she said, walking toward the young man I assumed to be her fiancé.

"Yes, I am," I answered, feeling much more tongue-tied than when we had spoken on the phone.

"This is Allen. Come on in." Once inside she maintained a safe distance from me as we stood in the foyer. Then, after what seemed like an interminably long pause, I followed them into the living room. There I was able to find my evasive tongue and say hello to Allen.

We sat on opposite sides of the room. I settled rigidly on a large beige couch, and my daughter rested across from me on a stiff, high-backed chair. Allen seemed the most natural. He actually moved an armchair closer to Rosanne, so that he was no more than a short reach away from her.

I was beginning to shake again. There was enough adrenalin pulsing through me to lift a house.

"This is a very nice place," I said, thinking how empty that state-ment was as soon as I had said it. I am not a "small talk" person, and yet now, face to face with my daughter, all I could do was commend a house I had barely looked at.

"Would you like something to drink?" Rosanne asked. Her ques-tion guided us both into amiable conversation and polite etiquette usually saved for strangers.

"Yes, anything at all," I answered, aching to ease our first moments together, but immobilized with anxiety. I was miles away from the perfect pictures I had imagined of this first meeting.

When my daughter and Allen left the room for a few minutes, I seized the opportunity to breathe deeply. I was, by then, visibly trembling, and each inhalation eased the tension. Tears were close, but I held them in, fearing they might shatter the fragile thread hold-ing me together.

Soon Allen and Rosanne returned with some cool drinks. Feign-ing calmness, I asked the question I so much wanted to answer.

"Do you want to know why I gave you up?"

"If you want to talk about it," she answered flatly.

Was she angry I wondered? Did she feel rejected by me? Was she masking her hatred? Where was the young woman who less than a year ago had expressed anger at being "thrown away"? What had she done with those feelings?

As I began my story, I prayed she would understand. Unknown to me then, what I really craved was forgiveness. But the full extent of my need was to surface only later.

On the afternoon of our first meeting, I told Rosanne of my love for her birthfather. I briefly mentioned the abortion attempts, all the while noticing that she appeared unexpectedly calm. I was not so much sharing my past as I was examining every facial expression, striving to match them with my expectations. I spoke quietly and apologetically, haunted by a need for absolution of my sins.

I shared stories about the wage home, her birth at the hospital and the lack of options available to me. All the while, she looked much too impassive, much too composed.

I hoped she would ask questions. But she did not. Perhaps she had genetically inherited the ability to retreat into an emotionally safe place. Did she have her own private tunnel?

We were a fine pair: she was enveloped in silence, and I was wrapped in guilt.

"I was amazed when your mother called me after seeing the newspaper article."

I directed this statement to Rosanne, wondering if it would trigger some remembrance of that fateful day when she refused to look at the folder revealing my identity.

"My sister had a baby that week, and my mother was spending some time with her," she replied.

There was not even a glimmer of anger. We were on different wavelengths.

"It's unbelievable that this accident of life allowed your mom to be in Fresno at that critical moment." I said, staying on this less-than-cozy theme.

"My father and my sisters were not in favor of our meeting, but my mother thought it would be okay," Rosanne said, momentarily leaving the protective shelter of risk-free communication, while I impolitely stared, attempting to uncover subtle nuances in her expression. There were none.

"I'm pleased your mom was agreeable," I finally answered, not realizing then how extraordinary my daughter's mother was.

"Do you have any animals?" I blurted out, at last accepting that a path lined with pleasant amenities was the best key to unlocking the tangled past.

"I've had many pets. I love dogs and horses," she answered.

"I'm more of a cat person. I can't imagine living without at least one or two cats as roommates."

"Do you drink at all?" Allen asked, breaking his silence now that we had entered safe conversation.

"I'm an easy drunk. One glass of wine and I'm almost asleep, so I don't drink much." They both laughed.

"Me, too. Allen calls me a cheap drunk."

"Perhaps it's genetic," I bravely added.

"I'm not much for small detail work like sewing, but I'm up to planting a tree," I continued.

Rosanne laughed again and shared her dislike of sewing as well.

"I've always had an interest in inexplicable phenomena. It was a remarkable incident that revealed Bakersfield as your location." I described my encounter with the man and his pendulum, hoping this was not a perilous topic.

Rosanne, engrossed in thought, looked intently at me and said, "When I was sixteen, and working part-time in a market, an old woman with a reputation for being weird walked up to me and said that my mother was looking for me."

"It certainly adds fuel to mystical occurrences," I said. "That was about the time I began my search for you."

A faint smile of wonderment flashed on all our faces as a temporary silence eased us into the secure arena of sharing more likes and dislikes. I learned that Rosanne had never cut her hair until her mid-teens. Her hair was still waist-length. I told her of my ankle-length hair and that it had been cut when I was thirteen. We thought it interesting that as children we both wore long, thick braids. We laughed at our penchant for gaining weight and our obsession with staying thin. We wondered if there was a genetic code programming this tendency.

"I work out and run almost every day, and I'm addicted to playing softball and soccer. That keeps the pounds off." She smiled, and I stared at her dimples, mesmerized by her beauty.

I observed a way of being—a determination—much like my own. Is this parental ego? This sharing and comparing satisfied us both. I had let the moment take its course and relaxed a little. We were breaking ground.

Children who are raised by their natural parents are slowly fused into discovery and comparison. Adopted children and their birth-parents are not. I fed an insatiable need as I watched her. Nineteen years of sensory deprivation faded as I sat with this young woman who was my daughter. Allen silently observed us.

Rosanne's next comment was layered with youthful cheerfulness. "I was hoping you'd be large-breasted, so I could hope to grow into some myself," she said laughing.

"Sorry, about that. I'm pretty small all the way around. Five-feet-two and one hundred pounds."

"I'm five-feet-three and ten pounds heavier," Rosanne looked at Allen, who was smiling.

"I love to hike and camp. Do you?" she asked.

"Yes."

"Genetic?"

"Who knows?" I smiled because she had used the word "genetic" this time.

"Would you like to meet your birthfather someday?" I bravely asked, hungering to move out of niceties and knowing I was re-entering heavier ground with my question.

"I don't ever want to meet him," Rosanne said, looking away from me.

I sensed anger in her voice.

"Would you like pictures of him?" I continued, knowing I wanted to get some photos of Karl to share with her.

"I'd look at them, if you had some." She spoke in a low, soft tone and then hesitated a second before continuing with what felt like newly-kindled irritation.

"It's getting late. My sister will be back soon, and I promised we'd be gone." She stood up quickly and looked at Allen.

"I understand," I said, wishing I had not mentioned her birth-father.

Then I quickly summoned up the courage to ask, "Would you mind if I take some pictures? I have my camera."

"Sure, Allen will take them. We can go outside."

I followed them both outside to a spot where Allen took several pictures, giving me the opportunity to stand close to Rosanne. Conversation did not spring up again. We were both stiff and unsure, but I was glad I would have photographs of this occasion.

When Allen returned my camera, I knew it was time to walk to the front where my car was parked. At that moment a stopwatch ticked in my head. And though there were no verbal signals guaranteeing ease, I hugged my daughter before my time ran out.

She seemed startled, or at least unprepared. Her arms hung limply by her side and then fleetingly brushed my back. Our awkwardness dislodged tears, which I quickly squelched. I did not want to cry. Not now. Not here. I turned and hugged Allen. He seemed surprised and did not hug me back.

I was a foreigner here, an interloper, an outsider.

"I'll send you copies of the pictures," I said, acting happy as I got into my car and drove off. They stood on the front lawn and waved good-bye.

Once in my car, a torrent of tears fell like an assault. Soon the tears were sobs, and then sobs became screams. The entire trip home was a journey of emotional purging. I was sliding down a long tunnel, with the end nowhere in sight. We had not really touched. We were still strangers.

9

Reactions

There are grand rewards for those who pick the high, hard roads, but those rewards are hidden by years.
—RICHARD BACH

My parents, who never really thought I would succeed in my search, were now looking at pictures of me with Rosanne. When I visited them a few weeks later, my father, who is not prone to serious discussion, looked at me and said, "I never thought you'd find her." Though his words were barely audible, his face screamed with astonishment.

Each requested that I not share the news about Rosanne with the relatives in Montreal. I did not do as they asked. I had defied society and succeeded. Now I refused to bury the fruits of my labor. I would not be stripped of my joy, bittersweet though it was.

My courageous rebelliousness enabled me to write and mail pictures to my numerous cousins, aunts and uncles. Without exception, everyone wrote back to express pleasure at the meeting with my long-lost daughter. All were solemnly taken by the miracle of it.

The ALMA and CUB newsletters printed my story. My friend, Barney, whose phone machine had held a tearful message of my daughter hating me, wrote:

An end and a new beginning as are all such moments.

A week after the visit to my parents, I received this note from my mother:

I look at the pictures every day and it is still so incredible! She is beautiful like you. I think it's the most wonderful thing that could have happened. We hope there is a new life to begin for you—a life of joy and happiness and of thanksgiving. I call it a miracle. So does your father.

It was evident that my parents' hardened beliefs melted at record speed under the reality of Rosanne's appearance in my life. Lee Campbell, founder of CUB, wrote:

We heard the wonderful, wonderful news of your reunion. I couldn't be happier for you.

My sister-in-law wrote:

I've thought about how I was against your looking for your daughter. Thank God you had the courage to continue your search. Seeing the pictures of Rosanne with you, and knowing how happy you are, I realize now that she was well worth looking for. I'm so glad you did not listen to our advice. This is truly a wonderful way to enter your forties. We have and always will love you . . . and now Rosanne.

I notified *The Sacramento Bee* about meeting my daughter, and they ran a follow-up story. At that time, only a few close friends on the staff where I taught knew about my past. I had no idea who would see the article, but I was curious about how my colleagues would react. The story appeared in the weekend edition of *The Bee*. It was a full page spread titled "Happy Ending." A four-by-six-inch photo accompanied the feature.

The story began:

A newspaper story, anonymous phone call, and lots of understanding helped her find a daughter she hadn't seen for nineteen years.

Louise Jurgens wanted to tell the story from the beginning but the ending kept getting in the way. Maybe it was because the ending she wanted to explain isn't an ending at all but a promising beginning that could help soften the pain still evident when she talks about the past. She wanted to talk about the series of coincidences including a story in The Bee two years earlier that led to her reunion with her daughter, the daughter she gave birth to nineteen years before, and saw briefly before signing the adoption papers she thought would separate them forever; the daughter she has grieved for ever since, and who has never been far from her heart.

The story was again handled with sensitivity and prodigious detail. It ended with my request that the anonymous caller be acknowledged.

"I saved the best for last," she said, and a smile that lit up her face chased the last shadow of the past away. "Rosanne is getting married next month, and I am invited to the wedding. I won't be going as part of the family, but I don't need to be. I'm just happy to be asked as a friend of the bride. I hope my anonymous caller will see this article and know how much I will always treasure that call."

The following Monday when I walked into the front office at school, one of the secretaries had the article and was passing it around. On the surface, it seemed that everyone was supportive and happy for me. Later, through the grapevine, I heard that a few staff members thought I had stepped on sacred ground, but none of them ever spoke to me about it. Within a few days no one mentioned the reunion, except those who applauded my search and shared a close bond.

My twelve- and thirteen-year-old students who were aware of the article were quiet for the most part. Many expressed delight or amazement that I was in the newspaper. I became a mini-celebrity in their eyes. It had little to do with finding my daughter.

There were a few who walked past me in the halls and said, "I wouldn't give up my baby."

The comments were never directed to me but were always spoken loudly enough for me to hear. My theater elective class handled this personal drama differently. For several days their improvisations exploded with adoption themes. In their less than subtle way, the children I taught touched me. I wished I could have been like the courageous, strong-minded, fearless women in their skits who, though pressured, never gave up their babies.

I continued to hear from friends, as more of them became aware of the reunion. These two letters reflected, in substance, many others which arrived daily for weeks.

> *I'm glad to finally know a celebrity. I mean, really, a full page! Not even the president gets that. I hope that you and your daughter will establish a good friendship. Congratulations!*

> *The biggest news of your life was a real miracle. When you were working to achieve it, I thought it was an exercise in near futility, but you're so tenacious about things important to you, I should have known you'd be successful. Please write me and tell me what you felt and thought. Will there be another meeting? How does your daughter feel about you?*

All my friends were concerned and very curious about what the future held for Rosanne and me. Personally, the change I expected to happen inside me did not occur. Meeting my daughter had definitely not healed my guilt. I became more conscious of it than ever before. I was also unearthing a mountainous load of regret.

When I received the wedding invitation in the mail, I needed all the strength I could muster to ready myself for this very public second meeting. My mailbox also contained a brief letter from Mrs. White with directions to the church. I was touched by her thoughtfulness.

During the next weeks, I labored under the delusion that I could do all of this alone. Had I anticipated the intensity of my reactions, I would have taken an army for emotional support that day. But again, I went unaccompanied.

On the morning of my daughter's wedding, I was once more locked in debate, attempting to decide what to wear. This occasion was to be more formal than our first meeting. Though not a high-fashion person, I am vain enough to select complimentary clothing. There is little in my sparsely-stocked closet that is not comfortable, yet attractive, and finding something to wear is usually effortless. But that day, I wanted so much to look extra pretty. Deciding what to wear was agonizing.

Not only would I see Rosanne again, but I would also meet her entire family and many of her friends. I was shaking so much, wondering what they'd think of me, that I could barely button the four outfits I tried on. None looked right. Finally, I chose a favorite old dress—it was a soft cotton in subdued earth tones. For the second time in my life, I had worn myself out just getting dressed.

I drove slowly, leaving hours before I needed to. On the entire trip down to Fresno my knuckles gripped the steering wheel so tightly that they turned white. Not surprisingly, I was early. Nonetheless, I went directly to the tiny, quaint church.

A photographer arrived just minutes after I parked. I stood by my car for a moment watching him. Almost immediately he asked if I was a member of the family. I told him I was a friend of the bride. He seemed unimpressed and disappeared into the chapel.

Soon family and friends began to gather. I stood by the open church door feeling ill-at-ease. Moments later, a handsome woman, dressed as only the mother of the bride might, approached me.

"You must be Louise," she said.

"Yes," I answered faintly.

"I'm Rose White."

She did not look like my imaginary pictures but very much like a nurturing mother.

"Thank you for the directions. They really helped." My throat was so dry that it hurt to talk.

"I wish I could have gotten them to you earlier, but it's been quite a week. Rosanne's dress did not fit right, and I had to redo a major portion of it."

"You sewed Rosanne's dress?" I asked, impressed with such skill and love. I suddenly yearned to hug my daughter's mother, but though only inches away, I stood motionless.

Unaware of my thoughts, Mrs. White continued, "Yes, and when she complained that the dress was too loose and made her look pregnant, I felt like giving her back to you."

I am not good at quick reparté and merely smiled, feeling stupid as I stared at this special woman.

Seconds later, a young woman in a long gown approached us.

"This is Rosanne's birthmother." Mrs. White's introduction was polite, but I felt the uneasiness in the air.

"I'm Susan, Rosanne's sister."

"Hello," I smiled, wondering if I should shake her hand or say something more. The decision was made for me as she quickly asked her mother to join her in the dressing room.

"I'll be back later," Mrs. White said as she followed her daughter.

I entered the empty church and sat quietly in the last pew on the left side, wondering if this was the official bride's side. I've never been good with formalities of this sort, but I wished I knew what was proper at that moment. I did not want to ask anyone.

Some fifteen minutes later, Mrs. White and another woman entered the church and walked over to me.

"I hate to have you be all alone, so I'm leaving you in the good hands of a dear friend."

Introductions were brief, and once again my daughter's mother left to care for last-minute details.

I was pleased and impressed that Mrs. White had taken time to take care of me. There was genuine warmth reflected in that act. I breathed in that feeling as a ray of light filtered through the stained glass windows and flooded the church with pastel hues. As I sat, not entirely without anxiety, thoughts of appropriate conversation with Mrs. White's friend escaped me.

The moment was punctuated when the woman sitting next to me said, "I have an adopted son, and he has no desire to meet his birthmother."

"Some adoptees never do," I answered weakly, stuffing my tears.

This woman's comment reflected everyone's concerns that day. Each carried his or her opinion of such a meeting, and each felt empathy for the problems I might cause the family and Rosanne. But, on that day, philosophical comfort escaped me as I sat waiting for my daughter to be married.

The ceremony was brief, and, though nervous, I was constantly aware of the miracle of being there. I was no longer in the maze—I was, in fact, munching on the best of all possible cheese.

Rosanne looked beautiful and radiant as she exited the church. When formal pictures were taken, I kept my distance, taking snapshots and comfortably staring, knowing my daughter was unaware that my eyes were glued on her. More than anything, I wanted a photo of Rosanne with me, but I was too intimidated to ask.

Once the picture taking was over, I began to feel out of place. My assigned companion tensely introduced me to several people, and each time I sensed discomfort with the word "birthmother." The unspoken communication, "What is she doing here?" permeated the air. It was becoming more and more difficult for me to keep my tears in check.

Thinking that I might start to cry uncontrollably prompted me to leave, but as I began to walk toward the car, I decided to grit my teeth and go to the reception. This was the first event in my daughter's life I had ever shared, and I was not willing to miss one second of it.

The reception was held at a comfortable, rustic restaurant. I sat at a corner table some distance from the main area. It was then, more than ever, that I wished I had brought a friend. Locked in my sadness, I felt seconds away from a flood of tears, but when Rosanne arrived, I was again captivated by her beauty and thankful that the crowd concealed my stares.

Watching from the periphery, I wallowed in self-reproach. I had missed my child's life. As I sat watching her with her family and friends, I felt a cavernous sorrow. Their love was evident throughout the entire affair.

I learned that her sisters had made the very professional-looking wedding cake. Many of the table decorations were made by friends and indicated warmth and caring. Envy and jealousy overwhelmed me as I smiled at strangers. All the while, an avalanche of remorse suffocated me.

After the meal Rosanne and Allen began to open gifts. When they came to the package I brought, my head spun in confusion. I had put together an album, labeling key relatives, grandparents and great-grandparents, and noting birthplaces and dates of birth and death. I included some favorite books and other personal items. My gift, sitting next to toasters and wine glasses, seemed inappropriate. I felt that these items might seem like an intrusion, highlighting my presence in a gathering where few were endeared with my being there in the first place.

In a panic, I stood up and quietly but deliberately said, "Please don't open that here."

Rosanne looked at me and put the gift aside. I sat down quickly, feeling conspicuous as the remaining gifts were opened.

Not long afterward, I noticed several people preparing to leave. I, too, wanted to go, but I dreaded moving. The table acted as a shield, making me somehow invisible, or so it seemed. When the couple to my left rose, I began to feel conspicuous and got up. Close to tears, I put my senses on hold as I inched toward Mr. and Mrs. White. Our good-byes were clumsy and stiff.

Rosanne and Allen were laughing with friends a few steps away. I hugged them both and thanked them for inviting me. We touched for a single, awkward moment.

I could hear the blood pulsing in my ears as I walked out. My only protection was the numbness I wore, but this masquerade dissolved as I sat behind the wheel of my car. All control slipped away, and tears again poured out in giant sobs and screams.

Earlier, I had promised my parents I would visit them after the wedding, not realizing that this would be incompatible with my emotional state. Proceeding as if my plans were etched in stone, I never thought to change my mind. I tried to block the feelings, but my heart could do nothing but ache.

As soon as I walked into the house, I wanted only to weep in my mother's arms. And, just seconds after I entered, I hugged her, sobbing all the while on her shoulder like a heartbroken little girl. She quickly broke our embrace, almost pushing me away.

We were unfamiliar with this type of intimacy. Through my tears, I saw she was more than uncomfortable—she looked terrified.

Both my parents are experts in emotionally suppressing the intensity of their own sadness. They were not prepared for my outburst. Experiencing my breakdown became very stressful. My father handed me a glass of wine, a rather loving but hopeless gesture.

My mother maintained her distance and kept repeating in a sing-song voice, "Everything's just fine. You'll see, everything's just fine."

It was late, and I felt drained. My tears were the only form of communication concerning the wedding. I was not coherent. My mother put me to bed with worry visible on her face. Sleep was fitful and interspersed with tears.

I left early the next morning. My parents probably understood my early departure—it's hard to know. We certainly did not discuss why I made such a short visit. I needed to be alone, and crying there was uncomfortable for all of us.

Once home, I made myself sick with regret. Rosanne's wedding had opened a flood gate of tears and buried emotion. It became clear that I desperately needed to stop the pain.

As I gained perspective, I knew I wanted Rosanne to forgive me, to say she loved me, to say she understood. But, it was beyond my comprehension at that time to grasp that conciliation would not come from her.

A few weeks after the wedding, Mrs. White mailed me a collection of the professional photographs taken that day. I had copies made and shared several favorites with my parents, friends and relatives. All but one of the snapshots I had taken were an indistinct blur. I was so nervous that day I had literally obliterated the lens with my thumb!

When my friend Michelle received the photos she wrote:

Dear Louise,

This is to thank you for sending the wonderful pictures of Rosanne's wedding and the article about your quest that appeared in The Sacramento Bee, *a very well-written story and in many ways as much a public service as a human interest article.*

You showed your usual high quality of courage in attending the wedding, and though it was hard, I know you're glad now, and perhaps will be even happier later that you went. No telling how close you and Rosanne may become in the future.

Love,
Michelle

My mother's letter came a few days later:

Dear Louise,

Thank you for the pictures of Rosanne's wedding. I know your feelings and love for her must be high, and you must be so happy.

*Aunt Mary called last night from Montreal. She loved the
pictures, too. She says Rosanne looks just like you—beautiful.*

*Well, Louise, tell Rosanne we love her very much—we
always did, and her parents, too. Tell her how we feel. She is very
beautiful. She is really the only one of our grandchildren who has a
resemblance to the French side of our family. I am proud of that.
Take good care of yourself. You have been through a lot of excite-
ment and anxiety these past months. Take it easy.*

> *We love you,*
> *Mom and Dad*

The sadness and regret cloaked in my mother's letter were
spawned in shame and fear. Once again these feelings might have
been a bridge to real closeness and love, but we were still disabled,
though at this point, I was beginning to see a flicker of light in my
private maze.

10

Search for Common Ground

Many men go fishing all of their lives without knowing that it is not fish they are after.
—THOREAU

A few months after Rosanne's wedding, I received a brief phone call from her inviting me to spend an evening that next weekend. I interpreted curiosity as the catalyst for her request, but whatever Rosanne's reason, all other aspects of my life paled beside my upcoming trip.

The little strength holding me together again crumbled as I deliberated about what to wear. It seemed that I needed to define myself for my daughter with my clothing, and on the morning of my trip to Bakersfield no amount of self-analysis could alleviate my heaviness. My selection of jeans and a loose-fitting, Indian-style top exhausted me. I wondered if I would ever be able to painlessly dress and accept myself on those occasions when I was to be with my daughter.

Driving south for five hours until I reached Bakersfield gave me time to defuse the time bomb ticking away inside me. I searched for a model upon which to base appropriate images for this visit. Television, books and movies had not engineered a reasonable facsimile for this situation. How could I develop a relationship with my daughter when we were almost total strangers? I felt like a trailblazer with no sense of direction.

I saw Allen and Rosanne in the front yard as I arrived. Walking towards them, my deepest impulse was to run and wrap Rosanne in a long embrace and thank her for having invited me. Instead, I calmly approached and gave her a fleeting hug. We touched like barely known acquaintances.

"How are you two doing?"

"We're fine. Come on in," Rosanne said, leading me into her home.

Once inside, I was warmly greeted by their dog and two parrots. The animal lover I am was in heaven. I so wanted to be able to say all the right things and share genuine feelings. But we talked instead about my drive down, the weather and the animals. I felt like I was in a Woody Allen movie with subtitles placed on the screen as my inarticulated dialogue juxtaposed with the inane conversation we were having.

"How was the traffic?" Rosanne asked.

"It was minimal, an easy drive down," I said, thinking, *You are so beautiful. Can I just stare at you for a few hours?*

"Who's taking care of your cat?"

"A friend will look in on him," I answered. *I can't believe I am sitting here with you in your home.*

"We just gave Bart a bath."

How do you feel about my being here? "He looks great." *Have you ever thought of what might have been?*

"He'll probably roll in the dirt in the yard and get filthy again."

We sat in the living room and talked about irrelevancies as my mind guarded what seemed like dangerous sentiments.

"My mom left these for you to look through," Rosanne said, pointing to several photo albums stacked on the floor next to the sofa. As I picked up the first one, my private monologue ground to a halt.

"Are these pictures of you?" Stupid question, I thought, once I had asked it.

"Me and my family. While you're looking at them, Allen and I will fix dinner."

"Can I help?"

"No, we've got it all handled."

As soon as my daughter and Allen left the room, I sat for a moment in awe of my daughter's mother's willingness to include me in Rosanne's life. I picked up the first of three albums and gently opened it. The occasion felt solemn. The young woman in the kitchen was transformed into a child in the photographs. I saw the baby I had surrendered for moral sanctity growing up with her family. My fingers flipped through vacations, Christmases, birthdays and Thanksgiving dinners. Each picture unalterably etched a profound regret.

The miracle of being with my daughter at this moment could not begin to sooth the undeniable reality that these moments captured on film were lost to me. I felt no anger, only an undeniable self-pity.

"I hope you're hungry for pizza." Rosanne's bubbly voice brought me back to the joy of being with her.

"Yes, I am. It smells great."

Much like the first time we met, our surest protection was found in the formalities of politeness, which fed the inconsequential but basic conversation that accompanied the meal. As before, questions I longed to ask took a back seat to talk about camping trips, school and jobs.

After dinner I watched the dog perform tricks, and was astonished at the parrots' vocabularies. There were thick walls to be penetrated before we touched who we really were. Perhaps, we were doing exactly what was needed in order to get to know one another.

Before bedtime Rosanne gave me a tour of her home. As she guided me through each of the rooms, I absorbed the pictures hanging on the walls, noticed the colors of bedspreads and fabrics and the beautiful antique furniture. These moments became a discovery, an illumined photograph revealing a tiny part of her. I had come a long way from my fear of being discovered as a birthmother to this moment. It was a true evolution—much more than a dream come true.

We ended in the kitchen, where I helped with a few dishes. Allen disappeared when Rosanne led me to the guest bedroom. We sat on the bed talking for a minute or two about how much she had loved her first horse. This topic was safe and led to a momentary hug as we said goodnight. This was the first time, short though it was, that we had been alone together.

As I pulled back the bedspread, I heard the dog being called to the bedroom. I have always felt that part of the joy of having animals is allowing them to sleep on the bed at night. I had discovered something else we had in common and smiled. I was no longer inventing a life for my daughter—this was more than secondhand information. *I'm in my daughter's home.* That was the last thought in my mind before I fell asleep.

The next morning, as the sun peeked through the curtains in my room, I dressed quickly and found Rosanne in the kitchen.

"Allen loves to sleep in," she said smiling.

"Let's go out for breakfast. My treat."

"That would be great!" she replied.

We went in her pickup. How odd life can be, I thought. Here I was riding in an unfamiliar vehicle, going to a restaurant in an unfamiliar city with my daughter. Everything in the past nineteen years had magnetically led me here, and yet I felt as fragile as a newborn butterfly.

Neither of us spoke during the short time it took to reach the restaurant, and once there our conversation was stiff, revealing an awkwardness and nervousness that was inescapable.

"What's your plan for the rest of the weekend?" Rosanne asked after we had ordered.

"When I get home, I intend to work on some papers that need correcting," I answered, suddenly awed by the challenge that lay before us—wishing there were shortcuts to intimacy. But, ancillary side issues, verbal busywork bounced back and forth across the table.

When our food arrived, the talk changed to sports. Other than gymnastics and ice skating, I have never watched an athletic game in my life, but I listened with as much interest as if I were a network jock.

We ate quickly and all of my desires to touch on a deep level vaporized with each bite of food, and each trivial topic of conversation. Keeping a safe emotional distance seemed the only certainty in our budding friendship.

After our meal, Rosanne drove us back to her place. We found Allen brewing coffee. I quickly withdrew into the bedroom and packed the few items I had brought.

Outside, I took pictures of Allen and my daughter, and he took some of us. I hugged them both, convinced I was trying to capture something just out of reach. This time, the hugs were less constrained, yet less than totally comfortable.

As I drove off, my mind burrowed into self-reproach. An ever-thickening cloud of regret was in conflict with the joy of having spent an evening with my daughter. I was limping into the future, while at the same time passionately focusing on my past. No matter how clearly I saw the beginnings of a developing friendship, I mourned the loss of my daughter.

Once home, nightfall sobered me. Wanting to continue my link with Rosanne led me to my desk where I composed a letter to her and Allen.

Dear Rosanne and Allen,

I arrived home midafternoon, where my cat met me at the door aching for attention. I gave him all he could absorb.

Now, after several hours of digesting our time together, I feel like writing. I hope this letter can breathe some clarity into my feelings which I want so much to share with you.

Looking at the albums and seeing you grow up in the pho-
tographs, happy with your family and pets, and realizing the mira-
cle of being in your home was awesome.

While sitting at the restaurant during breakfast, I was pro-
foundly aware of the gift of knowing you, but I sensed we were both
nervous.

Tonight my insides are singing, "I was with my daughter,"
and though I experienced phenomenal joy being with you, my feel-
ings are layered with images of the past, seen as replete with mis-
takes.

It feels paradoxical to know such happiness and yet be
aware of an undercurrent of sorrow as well. It is as if I am living my
dream but have yet to absorb it.

Perhaps we can get together again in the not-too-distant
future and go camping. Have a good tomorrow, both of you. See you
whenever we can do it again.

Love,
Louise

I was no more able to articulate that I hungered for forgiveness in writing than I had been in her presence. My letter was an extension of my frustration.

After that visit, we did not see each other for close to a year. I feared appearing I was trying to bulldoze myself into her life, so I only called occasionally or wrote cards and letters.

When summer rolled around, I phoned and suggested we go camping together. I thought that if we met in neutral territory it might be easier for both of us. She agreed with little hesitancy. I was overjoyed with her quick response. We decided to meet at the central headquarters in Sequoia National Park.

On this occasion, I invited someone to go with me, thinking I would get support, and it would be more relaxing for Rosanne to relate to me if I were not alone.

I asked Fred, an acquaintance who I knew loved camping, to join me. Unfortunately, his mastery of the wilds was equal to his inability to provide emotional support. But in those days, I was an amateur at recognizing kindness.

Our situation became challenging the minute we arrived and discovered that there were a minimum of ten central stations. Each was twenty to fifty miles apart and each managed hundreds of campsites. I didn't know which one Rosanne had selected.

Undaunted, I had no intention of leaving until I found her in this park, huge though it was. I had found her under impossible odds. I had no doubt I would find her here.

I called each central post and asked them to check for messages. Fred quickly got bored. He suggested we set up camp for the evening and hike around the next day without Rosanne and Allen. Undaunted, I kept calling until one of my calls hit pay dirt. Rosanne had left a note. The news quieted Fred for a moment.

When we arrived at the correct campground, I learned it was at least ten square miles. Rosanne could have been anywhere. Again, Fred was discouraged and suggested we find a place and forget about finding her.

"I can't give up now. We're so close. We will find her." I began to wish Fred would disappear.

"There are miles of spots. She might be out of sight from the road. What will you do when it gets dark, walk around with a flashlight?"

"If I have to, yes." There was no one who could have talked me out of finding Rosanne.

I visualized her with long braids and calmly told Fred we would drive around the paths until I spotted her. We set off and two minutes later I spotted her crossing the road. Her hair was braided.

I soon learned that Allen had also assumed we would never find each other.

Rosanne said, "I told Allen that you had found me under more difficult circumstances and you'd find me here."

That was a direct acknowledgment from Rosanne—a validation of her pleasure that I had persevered and found her. I ached for that acceptance—that approval from her.

Sequoia was spectacular. We hiked and took pictures next to majestic trees. Rosanne displayed agility and comfortableness with hiking, while I discretely stared, melting with each dimpled smile. That evening after we had all slipped into our sleeping bags, I marveled that, once again, I was with my daughter. I looked at the stars and thanked God for another gift, as I fell asleep listening to the sounds of the wind in the trees and the crackling of the campfire.

The next morning while we ate breakfast Rosanne mentioned that she had evening commitments in Bakersfield. So, we hiked until midafternoon then packed our gear.

As we drove off, I was consumed with the sense of losing her all over again. Fred soon began endlessly talking, comparing Sequoia to other national parks while I held in my tears.

The belief that my life would be joyously transformed when I met my daughter was not happening. Blending my past with the present and then creating the future seemed the only journey I could take. However, I had no idea how to construct that map.

The following year, on my fortieth birthday, close friends and colleagues at work urged me to celebrate with a small party. The gathering was planned at a friend's country home.

I wrote to Rosanne and invited her. My parents, both of my brothers and their wives and one of my cousins and her husband drove up from Southern California. The biggest surprise was that Rosanne called to say she would be there.

I was expecting her to bring Allen, but she arrived at my door with a girlfriend an hour before the party was to start. I guessed that the relationship with Allen was not going well, but I did not broach the subject as I gave them a brief tour. Now, it was my turn to share my home. I let them know they could use the bedroom and I would use the couch.

She and her friend quickly changed for the party, and then Rosanne suggested she follow me to my friend's house. We had barely talked and now we were on our way in separate vehicles. Not exactly what I had pictured, but it was nevertheless an exhilarating continuation of our developing friendship—a giant step forward.

When we arrived at the party, she met my friends, my parents, my brothers and a cousin. I could sense that the gathering overwhelmed her. I did what I could to ease the confusion, but she was uncomfortable and shy.

In less than an hour she asked for directions and the key to my place. It was not the best way to have everyone meet Rosanne. I had led her into my old maze with no directions and no cheese. Where was my power to protect her?

Incapable of providing comfort, I gave her directions and the key to my house. As I watched my daughter leave with her girlfriend, I felt hollow. I wanted to go with her, but instead I mingled with friends and relatives knowing it would have been ultimate rudeness to leave a party planned for me and attended by many who had driven over four hundred miles to be there.

Later that evening, when I arrived home I heard nothing. She and her girlfriend were asleep. As I quietly prepared the couch for sleeping, I strained to hear a sound from the bedroom. Only my cat joined me. I stroked his head as he cuddled on my lap. My daughter was in my bedroom! I restrained an urge to go "tuck her in" before I fell asleep.

The following morning had been organized by my dad. He arranged that we meet at a specific restaurant for breakfast. Rosanne and her friend packed quickly. Again, we drove in separate vehicles. Again, she followed me.

The family contingent was there, and I could sense that Rosanne was edgy. We probably all had an emotional hangover. Luckily, my father's extroverted personality eased the gathering. He told jokes and everyone laughed, yet I also sensed the presence of fear. I saw it in my mother's face and in Rosanne's, though we all looked normal enough on the surface. There was love there, too, but I had an eerie feeling that once again I was navigating blindly. How do I enter these unchartered waters? How do I make it safe and easy for my daughter?

The breakfast went well. Ironically, it was my dad's smooth repartee, and not my silence, that softened our shells. My father, who had followed society's lead to hide the existence of this child, was now warming her heart with his banter.

After the meal, everyone exchanged awkward good-byes with Rosanne, and drove off to their respective homes. A few days later, I received this letter from my mother.

> *Dear Louise,*
>
> *It was a lovely party. Your friend and her husband are really fantastic friends. Their house is charming and everything went well. You looked beautiful as you always do and, of course, Rosanne was lovely.*
>
> *I wish I could have talked to her, but it was difficult because she is very shy. It was not easy at the party to start a conversation, and she left so early. Then at the restaurant it was almost impossible to talk across the table.*
>
> *I hope she liked us and will come down here sometime. We are very happy that you finally met. I believe it was not that difficult.*
>
> *Love,*
> *Mom*

I knew there was love in my mother's words, but I felt her sorrow as well. The last sentence roused a sad smile. How I wished she had the eyes to really see or the strength to voice her grief.

A few months after my birthday party my younger brother, Frank, was killed in an automobile accident. His unexpected death was a crushing blow to the entire family. I called and shared my brother's death with Rose and Rosanne. Both were deeply sympathetic.

A few days after my brief conversation with my daughter she mailed me Susan Power's book *Thinking of You in Your Time of Need: A Treasury of Thoughts and Verse.* The inside cover held four precious words, "All my love, Rosanne."

This letter followed a day later.

Louise,

I remember your brother, Frank, from your birthday party. He was a beautiful person. I can imagine your sadness. The saying "Time heals all wounds" is true.

Right now I know your sadness is deep within you and there is still a lot of hurt and questions. Why him? Why that way? I can't tell you, you'll find the answers in time. You can learn from this as you already have. Sometimes it seems to take a deep sadness and hurt to become more aware of yourself and others around you.

Don't worry, life will be happy and "good" again. Keep your chin up, there are a lot of loving people around you. Take care and write soon.

Rosanne

She revealed more in her letter than she knew. Her words were soothing beyond description, communicating a wisdom and gentleness that lightened my heart.

11

Forgotten Tears

> *I must endure the presence of two or three caterpillars*
> *if I wish to become acquainted with the butterflies.*
> —ANTOINE DE SAINT-EXUPÉRY

Outwardly, all seemed to be rolling along as smoothly as possible. However, it was one thing to appear acquiescent and altogether another to harbor repressed needs surfacing for air without warning. My newly awakened adult was about to take an unplanned pilgrimage into the past.

I was in Southern California a year after my brother's death. My visit started out routinely enough, until I arrived at a small family gathering Edward had arranged at his home for vacationing relatives.

These old friends and a new adult cousin witnessed an emergence of courage in me that no doubt amazed them, perhaps as much as my behavior stunned me. Just seconds after stepping into the living room, my father's tortuous introduction slapped me out of years of somnambulism.

"This is Louise. She's got such small breasts that they're growing on the inside." He waited for the usual laughter, but for once there was none.

Then, unbelievably, in that next second I heard myself say, "Dad, I really hate it when you say that. I always have. It hurts my feelings and embarrasses me."

I cannot recall what the others did or said. I took a deep breath and watched my hands shake, as my life flashed before my eyes with technicolor, stereophonic force. This only happens when you die, I remember thinking. It was my father who jarred me into the present.

"Well, go to hell then," he angrily whispered, as he rushed into the kitchen.

My brother walked up to me and said, "Don't take anything he says too seriously."

"As a child I took everything seriously, Edward. I'm only now beginning to see other possibilities." I was crying but the tears felt good. I was no longer my father's to sacrifice for laughs. I had regained some power and won a fearsome battle.

Soon the family pushed aside this unexpected upheaval, and dinner offered a cleansing of all misdeeds. Reconciliation was not an issue. My father redeemed himself by never introducing me like that again. What might have been, I wondered that day, if I had possessed such power as a child.

On the day before I left to return home, I was intoxicated with my newfound strength and ready to release another inner demon. It seemed that this particular visit with my parents was divinely organized to inspire me with courage.

I had long desired pictures and a health history of Rosanne's birthfather's side of the family, and now infused with valiant resoluteness, I called Karl's mother. She was still listed in the phone directory, and he was not. One more brick cementing me to my past was to be loosened. I told no one about the call.

As I dialed, my mind raced ahead, forming pictures of a warm visit and shared delight in the miracle of having met my daughter. I naively assumed Mrs. Cabigon would want to get together and share my joy. A woman answered.

"Hello," I said, "this is Louise Jurgens. It is difficult to know where to begin." The woman listened quietly.

"Are you Karl Cabigon's mother?" I finally asked, gaining some clarity.

"Yes, I am," she answered.

"Twenty-two years ago, I gave birth to a daughter. I was Louise Antognoli then. She is Karl's daughter, too."

There was dead silence on the line, and yet I was certain she was still listening.

"I'm in Southern California for a few days visiting my parents. I was wondering if I could stop by and pick up some photos of Karl's side of the family to share with my daughter. I have photos for you, if you'd like them. I'm hoping we can meet, even for a few minutes. I can imagine that you might have many questions."

I knew I did not want to discuss the details of having found Rosanne over the phone. I assumed Mrs. Cabigon had no knowledge that I had surrendered my child to adoption. Most likely, the last time she had direct contact concerning me was when my parents drove to her home to force Karl to marry me. I momentarily froze, doubting the appropriateness of my call. But I continued, not knowing how to extricate myself at this point.

"I am also interested in a health history on Karl's side of the family."

The silence upset me. This is not the way to handle this, I thought. I scolded myself wondering how I could properly talk to my daughter's birthgrandmother.

"Karl had all the usual baby diseases. He's been very healthy." Her voice startled me. She was brusque, but I was pleased to get any reply by now.

"Can we meet for a few minutes?"

Something propelled me to follow this path, feeling that it would be easier for both of us if we talked face to face.

"We can discuss anything you need over the phone." Again I sensed resistance. "My husband and I were divorced when Karl was very young. I don't know anything about that part of his life. There have been a few heart attacks on my side of the family, but for the most part everyone is long-lived. If you want to know anything else, I suggest you call Karl."

"I would not have bothered you, except that you are listed and Karl is not," I replied.

"I can give you Karl's business address and phone number. You can call or write him there. He is married now." Her voice was sharp and left no opening to comfortably discuss my reunion with Rosanne, so I chose to hold in my frustration, thankful that her sharing would now allow me to contact Rosanne's father.

Just before she hung up, she asked, "Is she pretty?" Her voice softened with this question, and all traces of anger melted. I was stunned and saddened by her inquiry. Those three words were so human and indicated such a personal, warm curiosity.

"Yes, she is very pretty. She has Karl's coloring and looks somewhat Eurasian. I will mail you some pictures."

"Thank you," her voice was a whisper.

"I'm sorry if this phone call has upset you. It must be strange to hear from me after so many years. I really appreciate the information you've given me."

"Karl's wife knows about the child." With that she hung up.

I sent her a thank you note and two pictures of Rosanne. She never wrote back.

When I returned home I decided to write Karl at work rather than risk calling him there. But what to write to my daughter's birthfather, whom I had not seen nor heard from since I had begged him to marry me over twenty years ago, baffled me. I thought I'd never set foot in his life again, but a maternal urge motivated me to create this small legacy linking my daughter to her ancestry. That singlemindedness helped me fashion this letter.

Dear Karl,

How's this for a voice from the past? Though not an easy letter to write, I am moved to reach backward in time to retrieve a gift for our birthdaughter, Rosanne. She was born August 7, 1961. The enclosed pictures are of her, me and her fiancé. They were taken to commemorate our first meeting.

I had never seen her before that day. Well, actually the last time I saw her she was five days old, when she was surrendered to adoption. The moral climate at that time was such that no other choice was possible. [Reading this covert apology, today, makes me cringe. Was I apologizing for not keeping her? To him?]

Years ago I began an intense search to locate her. I have no other children, and I wanted to know if my daughter was alive or dead, happy or sad. Mainly, I had a deep need to meet her.

The story of how I located Rosanne and the peripheral relationship I am beginning to develop with her is unique.

A set of miraculous accidents guided me. I'll relate them to you if you're ever interested. It's been a long adventure across California, one that earns me the title "Sherlock Jurgens"!

Not too long ago I spoke with your mother on the phone in an effort to get a health history. I had hoped to speak with her in person about my search, but we never got together. I was reluctant to disclose the whole story over the phone. I did get a partial health history and your mother gave me your business address and phone number. I chose to write to you because calling seemed too bizarre, much like walking up behind you, putting my hands over your eyes and saying, "Guess who?"

At any rate, the purpose of this letter is twofold: one, to send you pictures of our daughter (I thought you might be a bit curious), and two, I'd like to request a picture of you and your mom and dad. I'm attempting to introduce Rosanne to your side of the family, at least in photos. Eventually, she might want to meet you. At this time, though, she doesn't.

She is truly beautiful. Her pictures do not do her justice. I've discovered she is a brilliant student, an expert pianist, athlete and horsewoman. She seems to be a gentle soul. I do not know her that well at this time.

Would you like to meet Rosanne? Do you know the whereabouts of her half-brother and -sister? She might be interested in meeting them someday.

I hope you can share in my joy of meeting this beautiful, young woman.

I assume you are well and happy and that you feel comfortable about contacting me. I am enclosing my current phone number and address.

I sent the same two pictures to your mother that I have enclosed for you. I felt she would enjoy seeing her granddaughter.

Please accept this letter in good spirits. I am eager to hear from you.

Regards,
Louise

Karl never responded to my letter. Undaunted and persistent, I wrote two more letters within a month. He responded to none of them, until one day, when he was far from my thoughts, I received a phone call.

"Hello," I answered. My voice met momentary silence.

"Hello, is this Louise?"

"Yes."

"Do you know who this is?" the caller asked.

I curbed my growing impatience, endeavoring to identify the voice I heard.

"No, who is this?" I asked, courteousness still reflected in my tone.

"This is Karl." My heart skipped a beat, which surprised me.

"Definitely a voice from the past." I forced myself to take a breath.

"I got your letters. I'm sorry I didn't get back to you, but my mother was very sick these past months. She died of cancer a few weeks ago." His voice was noticeably pensive.

"I remember how much you loved your mother. I'm sorry."

"I've never been so shaken by anything before in my life. We were very close."

"Death is difficult to digest. Time will diminish the pain but that doesn't help right now." I knew my valiant efforts to soothe Karl's sadness were futile, but I felt a need to comfort him.

"I really couldn't get into your letters, but I will be sending you some pictures. I don't have any of my father at the moment, but I have some of me and my mother."

"I'd really appreciate that." I wanted to ask him about Rosanne—if he ever thought of her, what he thought of her pictures. But I said nothing. My questions faded into some unknown fear, and politeness replaced my curiosity and buried anger.

"I'm beginning to look through my mother's things. Maybe I'll find a picture of my dad. I'll get it all to you in a couple of days."

He volunteered no further information.

"Could I have your home address and phone number?" I asked almost apologetically.

He gave me his address and number. As I wrote, I was aware that what strength of purpose I had melted hearing Karl's voice. I was hurled back into my maze.

"Well, then," he said after a brief pause, "good-bye."

"Good-bye, Karl." I hung up the phone, wondering why this unexpected call had immobilized my tongue.

I did not think of Karl after that. Separation from my feelings was all I could handle. Having talked to my daughter's birthfather seemed anticlimactic to finally knowing Rosanne. I rested in the belief that I would get the pictures. Months passed. I never heard from Karl again, either by mail or phone.

That summer, when I was in Southern California visiting my parents, I decided to call him. I have not always been consistently brave, but I am always persistent. This was unfinished business, and I wanted the pictures for Rosanne.

The call was covert. My parents were not overly fond of Karl, having never resolved their anger, so I thought it best to conceal my plan. At that time, I was one step behind them. They at least knew they hated him, while I had no idea that I harbored a colossal rage.

My trembling fingers worked against me as I dialed his number. That should have been a clue, but it was not. It did not occur to me to think of anything but the pictures.

The phone rang three times. Karl answered, and our conversation was brief.

"This is Louise. I'm here visiting my parents. Can we meet for a minute so that I can get the pictures?" There was no hello, no how do you do. I was not so much uncivil as tense.

"Okay, how about tomorrow afternoon at three?" I was pleased, and yet astonished at his quick compliance. He selected a restaurant. It was near his home.

"I'll be there."

My close friend Joan had accompanied me to Southern California. I shared the call with her.

"Do you know where this restaurant is?" she asked.

"No, I'll ask my brother. I think he can handle the meeting." Edward surprised me. Pleased that I would get pictures for Rosanne, he decided to accompany me, as did Joan. We were all naive, expecting a quick hello, collection of a few pictures and a brief visit. Looking back, I am amazed that I was not aware of the emotional turmoil seething inside me.

Karl was not there when we arrived. As we waited, Edward bought me a chocolate liqueur, which I inhaled. Both he and Joan looked at me and simultaneously asked, "Are you okay?"

"I think I'm nervous. Can I have another?"

"If you promise to sip this one."

I downed the next drink as quickly as the first.

"That's all you get." Edward looked concerned.

Though definitely feeling the two drinks, there was no repression possible that next instant when I saw Karl walk in.

"We'll have coffee while you two talk," my brother said. I paid no attention to Joan and Edward as they left.

Karl's once dark brown hair was almost totally gray. He noticed my stare as he walked up to me.

"Little grayer than you remember, huh?"

"Yes, you've changed some."

I followed him to a corner booth in the bar, comforted that I was sedated with the alcohol.

"This is an old haunt of mine. Everybody knows me here." He seemed relaxed as he hailed the waitress and ordered himself a drink.

"Want something?"

"No, I'm pretty woozy already."

"One more won't hurt. Give her another of whatever she was having." I didn't stop him. The waitress smiled and left.

"It's been a while, huh?" He leaned back and lit a cigarette. I did not stop him even though I am allergic to smoke and have learned to ask that small politeness of others.

I watched Karl pull an envelope from his pocket and place it in front of me.

"The pictures," he said. "Couldn't find any of my elusive father, but I got some of me and my mother."

I opened the envelope and looked at a young Karl with dark hair. His mother smiled at me in the pictures.

"Do you remember what I used to call you?"

"I don't recall," I honestly said, trying vainly to retrieve a phrase or comment from the past.

"My little angel." He looked stunned that I had forgotten.

"When I got your letter and saw you next to our daughter I said, 'That's my little angel.' "

"Oh, I remember now." I lied, feeling mesmerized by him. Simultaneously, I was staggered by the realization of how totally I had blocked any thought of this man for over twenty years.

"I haven't changed much. I still like a good time." Karl spotted a friend across the room and yelled, "Hey, Rob, this is my lady." He stood and shook the man's hand when he reached the booth. "She's the mother of our kid."

"Hey, man, outta sight." The man walked back to the bar. I felt eighteen, shy and awkward.

I managed to ask, "Do you have any children?"

"My wife has a daughter. She's got my name. I have a girlfriend, too, always have." He seemed proud of himself.

"Want one?" He pulled some pills from his pocket.

"What is it?"

"Speed. Keeps me going."

"No thanks," I said, as he put one on the napkin next to my drink.

"For later, you might want it," he said, quickly swallowing his.

I battled for a small semblance of composure.

"Would you like to meet Rosanne someday?" I asked him.

"I'm never going to go to her, but my home is open if she wants to visit. I've always got some good dope on hand."

Even in my stupor, my maternal, protective instincts piqued. I hoped Rosanne would never want to meet her birthfather. Roused from years of unconsciousness, I wondered who the eighteen-year-old was who had so loved this man.

"You're still looking real good. You'll always be my little angel." He held my hand. I did nothing, hypnotized once more.

"We'll be together again, I'm positive." He laughed. "You know, you live in my old stomping grounds. I used to hang out at Lodi Lake and get into trouble when I was a kid."

"You used to live in Lodi?" I was dumfounded.

"No, just a stone's throw away in Stockton until we moved here. Small world." He laughed again, looking very pleased.

My nervousness hid the question I ached to ask. Then, pushing through my paralysis to find an unexpected wellspring of courage, I inquired, "Do you know the whereabouts of your other children? Your son and daughter?"

Karl took a long, slow drag from his cigarette and said, "I don't know where they are." I had anticipated a pause, some reaction, but his demeanor remained unruffled. He stared at my liqueur glass which was still full and he ordered himself another drink.

"You're a lightweight. My old lady can keep up with me and she doesn't drink melted candy bars." His wide-mouthed grin irritated me.

My mother was right to hate this man, I thought. I considered the ramifications of a marriage to Karl and shuddered, surprising myself with my accelerating anger.

He lit another cigarette and talked smugly about his new car, his house, the easy hours at work. He smoked one cigarette after another and drank enough to have easily rendered me unconscious, if not dead.

The smoke was growing more uncomfortable, but I said nothing. I did nothing. In a million years, I would never have predicted my reaction. What I experienced was a bond. I was with the father of my daughter. My growing malaise paradoxically took a back seat to feeling this link.

So I sat on my anger and listened, wondering if he'd ever consume enough alcohol or drugs to permanently liberate him from his inner struggle. How much longer, and at what price, could he keep his past submerged? Would he ever escape from his self-created nightmare? Could a psychoanalyst extricate him from his fears? And where was I right now? I had unearthed bits and pieces of my past, but how much more was there?

I looked at Karl. He was not what I had hoped to find for Rosanne, but I would soon learn that this meeting held a key to the disengagement from one of the darkest, most tangled parts of my maze.

Edward and Joan extricated me from my thoughts. "We've got to be going." Their synchronized voices surprised me. I had forgotten them.

"All right," I said, "Just another minute." They nodded and left.

Karl finished the drink in front of him, and then moved closer to me. "We'll have one more time together, you mark my words." The form of our meeting changed as Karl suddenly pulled me into his arms and kissed me. At one time I would have given my life for this man, but at that moment I pushed away from his hold and looked for Joan and Edward. I needed saving. Fortunately, I saw them at the door. I left Karl at the booth, knowing I would never see him again. I said nothing, not even good-bye. I ran to the door.

As I followed Edward and Joan to the car, buried grief exploded in my face. I was not prepared for this reaction. None of us were. Both hugged me and attempted to sooth me with comforting words. I frightened myself because I could not control my sobs.

Once in the car I heard Edward and Joan whisper, "We can't take her home like this."

Joan asked me for Michelle's phone number. They stopped at a phone booth while I continued to weep.

Joan and Edward returned minutes later, looking worried. "We think it would be good if you went to see a therapist." Michelle suggested one near here.

"I don't care," I said through my tears.

They drove me to a psychologist's office. Once there, I met with a kind woman who was sympathetic and helpful. I spoke with her for two hours, unraveling years of stored anger and allowing feelings of rejection to surface for the first time. This session was a compelling beginning to my healing and helped me simulate a semblance of normalcy that last evening with my parents.

Joan and I left the next day. She soon grew accustomed to my weeping. Tears began at the merest thought of Karl. I had crawled into my past, only to cry for someone I hadn't thought of for over twenty years. Another sealed door was now open wide. Was there a divine power that led me to this face-to-face encounter with Karl? He could have mailed me the pictures, but he had not.

Had I followed my heart that day, I would have gone straight home, but I had promised Rosanne I would stop for a short visit, not knowing then that I would be in such a state. I hoped my tears could be squelched long enough to share the pictures that had scarcely cooled in my pocket.

When we arrived at Rosanne's, her mother was there, too. It was she who most eagerly absorbed the photos, but seeing Rose and my daughter made me regret the fact that I had stopped. Tears were close.

"Do you know what part of the Philippines Karl's father came from?" Mrs. White asked.

"No, I don't know anything about him," I said, pleased that her question momentarily distanced me from my sadness.

I noticed Rosanne was only marginally interested in the photos, while Rose was genuinely curious and eagerly studied each one, indicating she wanted to know more about her daughter's genetic past.

Allen was in the kitchen. He never came into the living room to say hello. Rosanne shared that her marriage was rocky. She seemed burdened and understandably distant, while Rose continued to scrutinize each photograph. Though I did not appreciate the depth of her interest at that time, it was to be of major importance in the future.

Soon my tears defied suppression. I knew the freeway offered safety, so with little grace, I made a hasty departure, hoping my daughter and Rose did not think me rude.

Rosanne and I were both crippled at this meeting. She struggled in her marriage, and I struggled to bury her birthfather.

I kept one picture of Karl. Looking at it or thinking of him launched me into unrestrained sobbing. Then, after two weeks, as if preordained through an act of God, I stopped grieving. All the anger and sadness had been washed away. Karl was not buried inside me any longer.

12

Towards Trust and Love

When an answer leads back to only one question, then you've hit the jackpot!
—FYNN

In a schedule forged in granite, further visits with Rosanne materialized only once a year. I'd write once or twice a month but the letters were one-sided. Time after time, I wondered if I should write at all. Even my sporadic phone calls were clumsy expressions of my love, often mired in mundane conversation. I knew I was at best only a peripheral friend.

During those years our visits were always short, often no more than one hour. Rose was always there and each time I became more and more aware of her presence. I developed a subconscious resentment of this, wondering if Rosanne was afraid to meet me alone, or if perhaps Rose wanted to check up on me.

As a change of pace on one of my stopovers in Bakersfield, I planned to meet Rosanne and Allen for breakfast at a local restaurant. When I arrived at the predetermined site, I realized it was the wrong place. Frustrated but determined, I drove to a phone booth and called every restaurant with similar names. I had no luck.

Having no option but to go home without seeing my daughter, I decided to call Rose. Luckily, she was home and extremely helpful. She knew about the breakfast and the exact restaurant location. She asked for the number and location of the phone booth and said she'd get right back to me.

A short time later the phone rang. Rose had directed Rosanne and Allen, who had by then finished breakfast, to another cafe in my area. Armed with new directions, I found them with ease, and though our meeting was brief and uneventful, I made a mental note about how helpful my daughter's mother had been. This was a small step into a hopeful tomorrow.

Soon after that meeting, my daughter and Allen were divorced. I kept writing monthly and calling a few times a year. Rosanne's main response was that she loathed letter writing. I knew this reunion game had no rules, but I hated inventing them as I went along.

My days hung together with self-imposed order until I was unexpectedly delivered into Rosanne's life with a call from Rose. She shared that three months earlier her only son had died in an automobile accident. She told me that Rosanne had been very close to her brother and had been so devastated by his death that she had not been able to work for a week.

I was shocked and saddened by the news on one level, and on another, I felt guilty that I had not phoned during the previous three months. I wished I had risked a communication or that my cards and letters had elicited a response. These thoughts crisscrossed my mind as I listened to a sad mother speak of her only son's death.

The call was short and ended with a profound and vulnerable disclosure. Before my daughter's mother hung up, she said, "I can begin to understand how you must have felt losing Rosanne, as she is your only child. Having lost my only son leaves me with such a loss. I assume you experienced the same pain with Rosanne. It is this realization that prompted me to call you." Her voice was soft.

I was deeply touched by her remarkable compassion. She shared that Rosanne had just moved and gave me her current address and phone number.

Minutes later I called her. Mention of her brother's death rekindled her grief. She sounded heavyhearted and sad. I wished I could have been there to hug and hold her, but I was not.

A sweeping realization hit me at this time. No analysis was needed to tell me that I was not an integral part of my daughter's life. I hovered in and out of her existence on an outer level only. Our relationship was marginal. She had not called to share her sadness. That was saved for friends. What was I in her life?

My question intensified my desire to become more than an acquaintance. Even though I knew I would never be her mother, I knew I wanted more than an expendable friendship. This presented a unique challenge and one I was not yet certain how to solve.

As I began looking for models I soberly realized there were none. It seems that society eagerly opens its arms to adoptive parents. They are blessed for their kindness. They are thanked for providing a home for a child. They are guided with readily available books such as *Adopting a Baby* and *Telling Your Child He Was Chosen.* No one sees them as recipients of a child taken from another.

Where was I to read about the best ways to incorporate a child surrendered to adoption into my life twenty-five years later? Where was I to read about the struggles of the birthparent or how to cope with the guilt of surrendering my child to adoption? Where was a map leading me into my daughter's life, so that I did not frighten her or offend anyone? Was that possible? Was my daughter satisfied at having met me? Did she want more? What had she done with her feelings of being rejected at birth? Did she feel angry?

Was I to spend the rest of my life in a new maze, hoping that by some magical accident all confusion would work itself out? I had no such faith. Indeed, finding her seemed less a miracle than ever before. The new miracle would be to begin a unique friendship. The answer was staring me in the face, but I struggled a while longer before I let it in.

Our pattern of visits remained the same except that I had, by now, mastered an effortless selection of clothing. What was unchanged was that each stopover lasted about an hour, and usually included my daughter's mother. I began to expect Rose to be there.

During one of our summer get-togethers, I arranged to meet Rosanne during her lunch break, as this was the only time that our schedules meshed. We planned to meet at her home. When I arrived, I was surprised to see Rose there. This was a lunch hour, a stolen bit of time for me to be with my daughter. Rosanne was almost twenty-six, and on this day Rose had arranged to rush there during her lunch break. I felt watched.

But gifts come deceptively clothed. This was to be the beginning of the second part of my miracle. As we sat and ate lunch, I awakened to Rose's intense inquisitiveness about me and my family. She always asked questions. Rosanne seldom, if ever, acted as if I was her birthmother. I was touched with Rose's guilelessness. She asked the questions I had always assumed, or hoped, Rosanne would ask.

The lunch was over quickly, and soon we were each off again. But this time, as I drove to my parent's home, my resistance to Rosanne's mother joining us when we got together began to look different. What I had been yearning for was embodied in my daughter's mother. I was motivated to write her regarding my observation.

Dear Rose,

I was not expecting to meet you at Rosanne's last week on my way down south. You always show a sincere interest and curiosity about Rosanne's genealogy. I always expected Rosanne to be curious, but she isn't, so I'm pleased that you are.

Perhaps because of what feels like incurable regret and guilt regarding Rosanne, I have a need to share about her birthrelatives. I have shared so little. Though I can see now that you have always been concerned, I was only really conscious of your interest when we were last together.

Whenever you want to see pictures or ask questions, please let me know. I find my relatives and their migration to Canada from various parts of the world an incredible journey of courage and determination. They are a colorful group of people.

    I don't know much about Rosanne's ancestors on her birth-father's side, but if you are interested I could possibly find out for you. At any rate, it was nice seeing you, and I hope your adventures are successful.

Regards,
Louise

I wrote a similar letter to Rosanne. A few weeks later my daughter called me. She said simply, "I'd like you to talk to my mother."

Rose got on the line and expressed a desire to meet my parents. She asked if that could be arranged. I was incredulously thrilled and told her that it could and that I'd get back to her. I received this letter the next day.

Dear Louise,

    It was nice seeing you and thanks for all the times you've written. Yes, I am interested in Rosanne's relatives for a couple of reasons. First, I have an intense interest in most people. I find that I can learn so much from personal associations that cannot be learned any other way. Secondly, I feel that one day Rosanne may want to know things about her ancestors, and it might be too late. As you know the young do not waste time thinking of time that is yet to be.

    Since my "baby" is twenty-six years old today I find myself thinking of many things, and it seemed to be a good time to write you.

    It is only when I think of the ages of my children that I realize that I, too, am getting older. Their birthdays are coming around much too fast. I frequently think of you, probably more than Rosanne does, because I feel that we share a common bond.

    Also, I owe you a debt I can never repay. After all, you gave birth to one who has given me years of pleasure. Many times I have wanted to suggest you stop over on one of your trips so we could talk, but I have been hesitant. I did not know how you would accept it and did not know if Rosanne would understand.

I find myself in a position of wanting to share Rosanne with you and not knowing how to do it without being pushy and without giving Rosanne the idea I am trying to push her away. Any ideas? If you ever want to call me please do. Thanks again for writing.

Rose

I read the letter and wept for all the needless fears we both had.

The next day, I called my parents and introduced them to the idea of meeting my daughter's mother. They were a bit skeptical and very nervous about such a meeting. Much to my surprise, they said they would get back to me.

I called Rose to obtain more information from her. She told me she would be going to Southern California in two weeks for job training. I shared my parents' address, and she was astonished that she would be in the exact same area. I called my parents again. They were downright scared and not at all convinced this was a good idea.

"Mom, Dad, this is such a massive breakthrough. It epitomizes a miracle. I see only positive results from your meeting Rose." My persuasiveness seemed futile.

"Why don't you just show her pictures of us," my mom logically said.

"She's seen pictures of you. Meeting someone is entirely different." I prayed that I could penetrate their resistance.

"It seems like you could just tell her about us." My mom did the talking while my father listened on the other line.

"That's not the same as being with you. Rose is curious about her daughter's birthgrandparents. She wants to know you personally."

"We'll call you later. Your father and I will talk about this a bit more."

My parents phoned six times in two days. Each conversation softened their resistance.

On the last call, my father asked, "What does she like to eat?" Eureka, I thought! They had resolved their struggle. This was really going to happen. All the details were communicated by phone. I was the backstage organizer, first calling Rose and then my parents to finalize the specifics. Ultimately, Rose and my parents were on their own.

My heart was cheered by the promise of an eventful occasion. Though four hundred miles away, a divine beacon soothed me. When the phone rang moments after Rose was driven back to her hotel, I was not surprised to hear the dinner had been charismatic, like pure silk from a spool.

I learned more about my daughter's adoption from my parents that evening than I had learned in the previous seven years. I believed that Rosanne had been adopted when she was five days old. Rose shared that they received my daughter three months after her birth. Bureaucracy moves slowly. Because I feared overstepping the imaginary boundaries of propriety, I never asked questions of this sort. It was my parents who now became the reporters of precious detail.

My mother related sharing photo albums full of relatives and was delighted that Rose brought hers as well. They genuinely enjoyed one another so deeply that another dinner was planned for the following week.

Later that same evening, Rose called me. She reported having had a pleasant visit, emphasizing her enjoyment of my dad's sense of humor and especially her pleasure at having browsed through albums of her daughter's birthrelatives. Tears flowed after each call, but these embodied an honest sense of joy. Because of Rose's bravery, all of our lives had changed course.

A few days after the dinner, I learned that my mother and Rose shared a unique sadness that evening, one that linked them in a poignant bond. When Rose looked at pictures of me with Frank, my mother talked about his death. Rose, too, spoke of her son's death in a similar accident. Each met the other's deceased son in pictures and shared a grief known only to them. They touched in a dimension beyond adoption and connected in their private sorrow.

Several days later I received a letter from Rose.

Hi!

> *Just a quick note. I had a lovely time with your parents last week, and I'm looking forward to a return visit. They are very friendly, concerned people. I was amazed to find they lived only a few blocks away from where I was staying.*

> *Rosanne has now agreed to visit them, and I am sure this will please them. Once she made the decision to see them, she seemed to become quite interested in the idea.*

> *She also made the statement she would have liked to have known your brother who died. She seemed to think he was a lot like the brother she lost. She still feels that loss.*

> *She appears to be somewhat concerned that your extended family may view her as an outsider and this may be why she has been so reticent.*

> *It was nice to hear from you. This course we are charting may indeed be very interesting. My main concern is for Rosanne, and I will do whatever is necessary for her continued happiness.*

> *If our relationship continues to grow, it should enhance our individual relationships with her. At this point in her life she seems to be ready to reach out to others, so she may be more accepting of your family. I truly hope so.*

> *Rose*

Rose was sharing concerns not revealed before. I was deeply moved. Her vulnerability carved a passageway for sharing love and friendship. The shackles of fear were loosening. I wrote back.

Dear Rose,

Thanks for your call and your letter. Your risking to share how you feel is a joy to me.

I, too, have not wanted to push myself into Rosanne's life, or yours. I feared I might offend you, or Rosanne, or your family, that it would look like I was trying to steal her away.

There are no models to observe or books to read guiding any of us who have traveled beyond the barriers within the adoption triangle. I sense we are trailblazers of sorts.

Thanks for wanting to meet my parents. I am glad you enjoyed being with them. I believe that due to the nurturing person you are Rosanne will never feel you are pushing her away. Thanks also for your warmth, openness and trust. I'm very happy Rosanne became your daughter.

Love,
Louise

There were more phone calls the following week to and from my parents' house. They were eager as well as nervous knowing my daughter wanted to meet them and that she would be joining Rose for the second dinner.

"We want to buy her a gift. Do you think that would be appropriate?" my mother asked during a particularly intense call.

I laughed and said, "Anyone over seventy need not ask permission to do anything they want." I heard a deep sigh.

"So you feel it would be a good idea?"

"Yes," I answered. "It would be perfect. Thank you for being so willing. You and Dad are both wonderful."

As I hung up, I was humbled by what I felt was God's creation of this "one of a kind" event.

I called Rosanne to tell her how happy I was that she was going to meet my parents. We agreed that although they had met briefly at my fortieth birthday party, this dinner was to be, on a conscious level, their first real meeting.

The second dinner went superbly. Everyone shared more photographs and comfortably grew to know one another. The meal extended into the following day when my father drove Rose and Rosanne around to window shop.

The visit smoothed away fear to such an extent that a few weeks after this dinner, when Rosanne had occasion to be in Southern California on a job-related training course, she called my parents. They met at a restaurant for another meal together.

Later that evening my father phoned. "She called—on her own—just to be with us again." His voice radiated pride.

"She is so beautiful and has such a joyous personality." My mother validated the wave of joy I heard in their voices.

It was exhilarating to hear my parents communicate such pleasure in knowing their granddaughter.

The journey into my daughter's life and hers into mine mushroomed after those meetings.

Three months later, during Christmas week, I arranged to have dinner in Bakersfield. When I arrived at the restaurant we had selected, I sat and chatted with Rose for over an hour, since Rosanne had been detained at work.

We relaxed together and talked about her avid interest in birds, especially parrots. She owned several and had bred a few, a very difficult endeavor, I discovered. The more I learned about Rose the more I realized what a rare and special woman she is.

When Rosanne joined us she brought a friend. We snapped a few pictures and exchanged Christmas gifts following our meal. My return home was peaceful and calm, so obviously unlike the partings of those first few years.

Soon after Christmas more surprises were in store for me when Rosanne and her roommate Judy made an unexpected visit on their way to the mountains. They spent an evening, favoring camping out on the floor in their sleeping bags to the offer of my bedroom. There was a continued growth in the ease of being together. My friend

Alice, who had often heard me speak of my daughter, joined us for breakfast the following morning.

At the restaurant I became aware for the first time since we had met that I was not staring at Rosanne anymore. The cavernous hunger to know her was being satisfied by the comfortableness of being with her.

A few weeks later, Rosanne called me again. "When it rains, it pours," she laughed.

"You won't believe this, but I'm going to be driving up your way again this weekend and I'd like you to meet a friend."

"That's terrific." I was flattered that she wanted me to meet someone she valued.

"We won't spend the night. We'll just stop to say hello."

This was becoming easy. As always, I was introduced as Louise, but juxtaposed with the introduction was the fact that I was her birthmother. This was clearly communicated when Rosanne dragged her friend to the bedroom to look at the wall-mounted pictures of her and her birthrelatives.

Staring at her yearbook photo, she asked, "Where did you get this?" She seemed awestruck. "That's my graduation picture!" She looked at me with a smile in her eyes.

"Before I ever met you, I ordered your yearbook and had an enlargement made of that photograph. I've had it on my wall ever since."

"No kidding," she said. "I didn't notice it the first time I was here."

That moment transcended the special friend she was becoming. I trusted she knew how much I loved her.

That year I received a Valentine's day card from Rosanne. It was simple, direct and powerful. She wrote:

> *Happy Valentine's Day. It's taken many years of not knowing each other and many years of getting to know each other to say, "I'm glad you're my friend."*
>
> > *Love,*
> > *Rosanne*

I carried that card in my purse for months. Other than the inscription in Susan Power's book, this was the first time Rosanne had signed a card with the word "love."

A week later my mailbox held more treasures. This time it was Rose who bestowed a gift without equal. The envelope contained a touching poem:

The Legacy of an Adopted Child

Once there were two women who never knew each other,
One you do not remember, the other you call mother.

Two different lives shaped to make yours one.
One became your guiding star, the other became your sun.

The first gave you life, the second taught you to live in it.

One gave you a nationality, the other gave you a name.
One gave you the seed of talent, the other gave you an aim.

One gave you emotions, the other calmed your fears.

One saw your first sweet smile, the other dried your tears.

One gave you up, it was all she could do, the other prayed for a child, and God led her straight to you.

And now you ask me through your tears, the age old questions through the years.

Hereditary or environment, which are you the product of, neither my darling, neither, just two different kinds of love.

My heart opened wide reading the poem. It represented not only one more facet of Rose's inimitable readiness to trust and include me in her daughter's life, but it also spread a nurturing blanket of acceptance over me. She had unlocked all the doors and put down a red carpet of welcome. I felt blessed by the benevolence of a higher power.

Unbelievably, more momentous events were on the back burner. On Rosanne's twenty-seventh birthday, I organized a dinner in Bakersfield with the help of my parents. This occasion was unprecedented because Mr. White joined us.

The first and last time I had seen my daughter's father was at her wedding. Over the years, Rose had shared that her husband was not against our relationship as much as he was a shy, solitary man—a loner who hated socializing.

I was pleased he risked joining us, luxuriating in the joy of our being together. Introductions were easy. As usual, my father's jokes picked up any slack in the conversation. Although the word "family" never came up, I felt we were all kin in our unique way. Mr. White's presence seemed like frosting on the cake.

After the meal we left to regroup at Rosanne's house. Her warm smile encouraged me to ask about baby pictures. "The albums I looked at years ago included no photographs of you under five or six," I said, "I'd love to see pictures when you were younger." I was pleased that I was now comfortable enough to request satisfying a longed-for desire.

"My mom has those albums," Rosanne said.

"I'll go get them." Rose said getting up so quickly she startled me.

"I thought they might be here. You don't need to go home for them. I can see them some other time." Politeness dampened my eagerness.

"I only live a few minutes away. I'll be right back."

While Rose was gone we talked for a while about Richard Bach's book *Illusions*. That was one of the items I had included in Rosanne's wedding gift, and I'd never known if she'd read it. Now I asked.

"I reread that book at least once a year. I love it," she announced. "You've turned me on to some great authors."

I smiled, pleased that time had ameliorated unnecessary fears. At last, on that evening, I was not afraid to be straightforward.

Soon Rose returned carrying albums and slides. As I made my way through the stack before me, I was quickly swept into the past—to that day twenty-seven years earlier when I gave birth to a beautiful, dimpled baby girl. I now, finally and fully, experienced the sensation of this little body in my arms—the photographs had provided the missing link.

This was a memorable gathering, certainly greater than a birthday celebration. More than friends, we held the budding potential of becoming an unparalleled family.

It was the cement of love that had motivated Rose into unknown territory, and it was her trust and courage that had eased us into the unit we were creating. Our birthday gathering was another serene monument to her mettle.

A few weeks after the dinner, Rosanne wrote me. I had given her another pair of favorite books, and she had lent me two in a collection of Jean Auel's books that I had begun reading. I felt a powerful intimacy reading books borrowed from my daughter. When I returned them by mail, I included copies of photographs I had taken on her birthday. They were the catalyst for a colossal acknowledgment from her.

Louise,

> *Wanted to say thanks for the books and for driving down to have dinner with me. I got your package yesterday. I'm glad you enjoyed the books I lent you. I did, too. I think everyone enjoyed themselves. Take care.*

> *Love,*
> *Rosanne*

> *P.S. Thanks for the pictures. It's amazing how much we look alike in them.*

This was Rosanne's first reference to a physical resemblance between us. Some of her resistance was softening. It was a link that made me smile.

Shortly before Rosanne's twenty-eighth birthday, the miracle expanded when she met my older brother and his family. Again, my parents were host to a dinner.

The catalysts for this fortuitous gathering were Rose and Rosanne themselves. They called and wanted to drive down to have dinner with my parents for no particular reason, other than to be with them. My mother lovingly and courageously suggested that the dinner include Edward and his family. Agreement was effortless. Buds were definitely blossoming.

Later, my brother called and detailed a friendly, relaxed evening. I phoned Rose and learned that my daughter had really enjoyed meeting her cousins.

Rose shared, "I don't feel I need to be there with Rosanne, but she seems to want me to accompany her on these first meetings. Perhaps she'll be able to go without me in the future."

"If all adoptive parents were like you, there would be no place for fear. I'm very happy that Rosanne has you to support her. You're a wonderfully loving mother," I told her.

The universe was showering me with extraordinary gifts. Equally phenomenal was Rosanne's flourishing friendship with my parents. A letter received soon after the meeting with Edward revealed her enthusiasm.

Dear Louise,

Hi! Wanted to send you a note to let you know I'm still alive and to tell you that you have some very special parents. I don't know if they told you but they let me and two friends of mine stay with them last Friday. They were so nice! They fed us all the time. I think we were there twelve hours and ate about five times!

I wanted you to meet these friends, but I couldn't get them to your neck of the woods. They're from Sweden, so I tried to show

them as much of California as I could. Take care of yourself. Write when you get a chance.

Love,
Rosanne

My parents called me a short while later and expressed their joy about the surprise visit. In a subdued, solemn voice, my mom and dad related that Rosanne had asked if they'd mind if she were to introduce them as her grandparents. They told her they would be honored, and when she did present them as her grandparents, they were literally overjoyed.

Quite an evolution here! My parents had gone from resistance to acceptance—then from acceptance to love. And now they were being called grandparents! I was a little jealous. Entering the picture more than twenty years down the road, my parents instantly became grandparents. I would never become mom. Not ever. As I said good-bye, I felt some residual regret. Perhaps it was envy.

13

Fragmented Miracle

Hatred is love without the facts.
—Richard Bach

We do not guide ourselves by hope. We guide ourselves by love.
—Richard Bach

By now, I had stopped my active affiliation with CUB and ALMA. During the period that I was associated with them, many members expressed interest that I write about my experiences. My close friends similarly hounded me. They had seen me progress from unconscious hiding, through struggle, to miracle—and all of them felt that the emotional challenge and triumph of this adventure begged to be shared. It was at their insistence that I began putting together a lengthy outline from my voluminous notes and files.

The first attempt to chronologically lay out my journey seemed more like an exercise in guarded journal writing than the birth of a story. I used a pseudonym and changed all identifying facts. The price of fear also led me to words that concealed a lingering uneasiness with sharing my private self. In fact, euphemisms sugarcoated much of the details, especially those regarding my childhood.

A one-hundred-and-forty-five-page outline sat on my desk for months. A close friend read my embryonic book and offered sug-

191

gestions, while I struggled to find time to continue writing. Another gigantic stumbling block stemmed from my intellectual insecurity.

But, once again fate was manufacturing its own script. The phone, which had been my champion from the beginning, again initiated the next step. This time Rosanne called to ask for help with a term paper she was writing for a college class.

"I don't know if I want to work this hard," she began.

"Going back to school can be tough." I attempted to offer some comfort.

"We've got to pick a topic for a term paper, and I selected adoption."

I was amazed that she had ventured into that arena. Indeed, I had always felt that Rosanne never truly felt adopted. She seldom, if ever, related to me as birthmother and at those times only marginally. So this term paper topic floored me.

"Do you have any material on the subject I could use?" Rosanne continued.

"Have you looked through *The Adoption Triangle* or books written by adoptees like *The Search for Anna Fisher*?" I asked.

"Yes, I have, but I need something more personal."

Her request guided me to my outline. I prayed for clarity as I clutched the phone like in the old days, and then a spark of courage moved me to say, "I wasn't going to share this with you, but I guess I will."

"You have something I could use?" she eagerly asked.

"Yes, you might want to read an outline I have written based on surrendering you to adoption and then finding you."

"I'd love to read it." She seemed to find no problem with this very personal subject.

"It's only the beginning of a book at the moment, and I've changed all the names, dates, and locations in order to protect everyone from public scrutiny." I couldn't believe I was talking to Rosanne about this, and paradoxically, I was elated that I could share it with her.

"Can you mail it to me? I need all the help I can get on this paper."

"It'll be in the mail tomorrow."

Her thanks and enthusiasm cheered me on but, at a gut level, I sensed a profound risk. Had I listened to my intuition, I would not have sent it to her. My naive expectations convinced me that if Rosanne read it, she would begin to see how much I loved her and begin to understand the inseparable bond I had with her. This belief moved me past my reticence. My friends thought this was a breakthrough, but it became a decision with mixed blessings.

As I placed my outline in a large envelope, I felt motivated to include a letter expressing my apprehension. My thoughts seemed unmanageable as I wrote to my daughter.

Dear Rosanne,

In response to our phone conversation, I am mailing you my outline, but I have mixed feelings about sending it to you. Letting you read about my reactions to all that has transpired in the past is frightening. Perhaps I am writing about experiences that should not be publicly shared. These fears motivated me to use a pseudonym and to change all identifying facts about everyone.

At any rate, I have dared to write about what I have felt and done, and I have dared to mail it to you. Eventually the outline will become a book and much as my friends have supported me to write it, they are now strongly suggesting that I use my real name. They are also wondering if, after you read it, you might give me permission to use your real name, actual dates and locations.

This outline discloses information and reveals interactions you may not be aware of. My logical mind tells me that the truth can never hurt. I hope I am not messing up our relationship by forwarding it to you.

Please share this letter and outline with your mother if you wish. Also, please let me know how you feel about it.

I think it could be a valuable contribution to millions of adoptees, adoptive parents and birthparents.
Eager to hear from you. Good luck with the term paper.
Much love,
Louise

Four days after I mailed the outline I got a call from Rose. My naiveté was in for a hard lesson as I listened. There was gentle caring in her voice as she told me that Rosanne had not been able to read further than page twenty-four.

"She froze reading about the abortion attempts," Rose said.

"The day she got the manuscript in the mail, she called me. I went to her house after work and read it that same evening. Rosanne began reading it later."

I was catapulted into a bottomless pit of grief as I listened to Rose.

"I mentioned the abortion attempts the first time I ever met her." My voice was shaky.

"She said she had never known about this before now. Perhaps she did not hear you then. I think she will read it through. She just needs to digest this for a little while."

How can she ever know how much I love her or even begin to understand the guilt, sadness and remorse I've experienced if she never reads past that section? I thought.

"When you first entered my life I had a profound fear and animosity towards you. Then I felt that Rosanne needed to be shared, that there was no sense not to trust."

Her words validated my previous conclusions, and I continued to marvel at the rare qualities inherent in my daughter's mother.

"I enjoyed the manuscript considerably." Her comment surprised me.

"It has a definite redeeming social value," she spoke slowly.

"Thank you," I answered, still glued to thoughts that Rosanne might hate me.

My biological tie had been my only opening, and now it had self-destructed in my face. What mother tries to kill her unborn child, fails, gives it away, and then seeks it out in love? What simplistic nonsense duped me into sending my outline? Again, Rose's voice jerked me from my thoughts into the present.

"Though I feel that your outline was most significant and merits publishing, I couldn't help but notice that you were a little hard on your parents."

All energy channeled to Rosanne collapsed with this comment. My mind suddenly raced in another direction.

"Perhaps you're right. I'll look more closely at that as I work on the book."

Rose's innocent-sounding remark quickly sucked me back into my need to appease other people's displeasure or criticism of me. It would take me four more years to realize how ingrained this pattern was.

As I progressed with my book, friends with whom I shared my manuscript stated that each rendering of the "Out of Childhood" chapter seemed authored by different people—one who clouded her past with euphemisms and yet another who described her early years with a sledgehammer. Each attempt to depict my childhood led me to thoughts of abandoning the entire project.

Looking back on those days I can see that this was my evolution out of one more dark chamber. I was only just beginning to understand my exaggerated need for approval, how I acknowledged my feelings through others and how angry I was. This survival behavior was extreme and required a deep incision into my very core. Each draft that ended up in the garbage sparked a renewed strength for honesty coupled with compassion.

I wanted to believe that my childhood was more or less normal. But the more I colored reality or my anger, the more congested I became. As I shredded page after page of distortions about my beginnings, I awakened my inner child to denial, anger, bottomless sadness and then, finally, I experienced a deep love for my parents. I saw that they had been injured by the pageant of their lives, and I realized that they acted in the most loving manner they could.

As the truth was forged as tenderly as possible onto the pages of my book, I wondered if my parents would be able to digest unlocking secret doors. I speculated about Rose and Rosanne's support of the truth about my youth. Was I willing to release my fear that their acceptance of me or of my parents might shift?

Obviously, I chose to transform myself with the truth, but it is love, not anger, that allowed my self-worth to emerge. I believe that my parents will eventually achieve an inner peace, though it is always an individual choice and challenge to evolve.

But, as I spoke to Rose that day, sorrow overwhelmed me.

"I can tell that you are sad about Rosanne's temporary inability to continue reading the manuscript. I do think she'll get back to it in time."

Rose's words scrambled my thoughts, and since I wasn't doing well in disguising my sorrow, I allowed tears to fall. Then, after a long silence, she continued.

"Your description of the time I presented Rosanne with your file was not handled as insensitively as you depicted."

I momentarily stiffened.

"I have no desire to write this story any way but truthfully." My voice was shaky, but I was able to focus on Rose's intent.

I asked her to detail exactly what happened that day in the kitchen. She did, and later I revised the scene to absolve her of responsibility for my daughter's reaction. Though she assured me that Rosanne would continue with the manuscript in time, I burst into tears as I hung up feeling that all gains up to this point had vaporized. Chaotic censure overpowered me. It was more than disappointment I felt—I was wrapped in a black cloud of fear that my daughter hated me and always would. My confidence was as shallow as my self-chastisement was deep. A measure of peace surfaced as I wrote to Rose after her call.

Dear Rose,

It was heartwarming talking to you a few hours ago. You are a very special woman. Thank you for your warmth, sensitivity and understanding.

At this moment, I feel so naive and stupid for having sent my manuscript to Rosanne.

Talking or writing about the past, especially the abortion attempts, is so challenging. It's hard to express, even now, how unworldly I was then. I thought Rosanne understood—I thought she had heard me that first time I met her in Fresno.

While speaking with you this evening, I felt closer to you than ever before and very undeserving of your care and concern. I have a profound, awesome respect of your love for Rosanne.

Please know I do not want to be in your life to cause you worry. It's never been my intention to burden you or her. I hope someday Rosanne can finish reading the manuscript, although I have no idea if that would make things better or worse.

I hope she will someday understand my behavior and find it in her heart to forgive me. Please let me know if I am needed in any way.

Love,

Louise

I continued to be stunned by my tears. All the knowledge I had acquired from reading books, attending seminars and working on my own personal growth seemed to be playing hide and seek with me. The depth of my sadness ran counter to all my expectations.

My friends' kind words could not penetrate my mood. Ultimately, it was my daughter's mother who touched me with her love and understanding.

Louise,

As I read your letter today, I felt your hurt and sadness, and I hope that by writing I can alleviate it somewhat. There has been too much ground covered and too many mountains climbed to have a major setback now.

Rosanne's hurt and anger seem to be subsiding. She has apparently given the situation much thought and she is again reading the manuscript—slowly. She said she expects to begin work in earnest on her research paper, and I'm sure that will give her "more food for thought."

As you know, she is quite intelligent and seems to have developed an insight far beyond her years. I feel she will work through this and emerge unscathed. When some of her personal pressures are removed, she will be able to relax and see everything differently.

You appear to be very worried that you have created problems. Relax, you haven't. When I first became involved in this triangle, I knew I was risking a great deal, but I felt you could only enhance and enrich Rosanne's life and should be given the chance. If I had felt otherwise, I would have acted very differently.

Needless to say, I feel that I was right and your presence has not had an adverse effect on either Rosanne or my relationship with her. I also believe that Rosanne has enough love to "go around" and I don't think anyone will be shortchanged.

If you still want to call her, you probably can now. I did want to reassure you, and I hope I have. As I said during our phone conversation I found your manuscript to be most interesting, and I think others will, also.

I have talked to Rosanne about the content of the manuscript and she said that you should leave it as it is. So you see, even if the truth hurts, that philosophy will help her through whatever comes.

As ever,
Rose

Rose's letter moved me past my tears. I came to grips with my self-imposed crisis of guilt by writing to her.

Dear Rose,

Thanks so much for your letter. You are very sweet. I continue being surprised at how sad I've been about Rosanne's struggle with the manuscript. I thought I was finished with feeling guilty and that I had "forgiven" myself. But when I realized that Rosanne was angry, I hated myself with renewed energy.

I really feel that somewhere there is a gift in all this. Suppressing anger is not healthy, and I know there is an anger that adoptees have about being "given away." I think it's time for Rosanne to get in touch with her anger, and it's time for me to really forgive myself.

Though this does not seem perfect, I know there is growth inviting itself for both Rosanne and me. Thanks for your love, wisdom and help.

Love,
Louise

It was time for me to write to Rosanne as well. I had heaped my thoughts and feelings so high that I was sure they would topple and crush me if I did not share them with her. That night I wrote:

Dear Rosanne,

I've been formulating a letter to you since I became aware that the manuscript stirred up "stuff" in you. Normally, I'm very good with words, or at least I can pen what I'm feeling, but this time there is no easy flow.

When we first met, that day at your sister's in Fresno, I blurted out my story. I had a sense you heard the communication about the abortion attempts but that you blocked the full emotional impact.

I had expected questions of some sort, but there was little change in your demeanor. I wasn't sure how to say what I wanted to share. I was definitely not able, then, to probe your stoic reactions.

Since then, as we've gotten to know each other, I've always felt that you've wanted to relate to me as a friend and not get into the reality that I am your birthmother. I know I cannot ever be your "mom," but to me you are more than a friend. I feel blessed with the miracle of finding you and knowing you on any level. So that role's been acceptable, especially when pitted against not knowing you at all.

Throughout the years I've met hundreds of adoptees. My best friend's husband Ron is an adoptee. Now in his forties, he searched for and found his birthmother about ten years ago.

He and other adoptees have spoken to me about experiencing a cellular sense of rejection and anger towards their birthmothers, no matter why or how they were surrendered to adoption. Often this emotion is suppressed and does not show up until they are older.

For Ron, that occurred when he was in his mid-thirties. He says he still gets bursts of sadness and anger to this day, although he "understands" why he was given up. That intellectual understanding does not, however, negate the anger and hurt. Part of me is glad that now, in your late twenties, you have gotten in touch with some anger.

When we last spoke and you mentioned writing a paper about being an adoptee, I felt this was an opportunity to open up that can of worms.

But since I mailed you the manuscript, I've beaten myself for being so naive. It was too much for you to digest consciously. At least, it seems so at this moment.

And now, I am asking you to take a sizeable leap into unconditional love. How can you possibly love me, knowing I tried to kill you in the womb and then surrendered you to adoption? Would that not strain even the loftiest soul?

I probably should not solicit your forgiveness. I need to forgive myself. I thought I had.

Your mother has been so lovingly helpful these past weeks. It has been her understanding and concern that helped to stabilize the renewed guilt and sadness that surfaced with this incident. If your soul had any choice, and I feel it did, it inscrutably pulled you into Rose's loving arms.

And now, most recently, you are becoming acquainted with your birthrelatives. The reasons for the long separation may not be clear to any of us at this time. Clarity may only be encountered on a spiritual level, but on a physical level I am, as you know, very happy that you are beginning to meet other members of your birthfamily.

I love you as a daughter and as a friend. I love your energy, intelligence, independence, strength, courage, spunk and wit. You are quite a wonderful experience in my life. See you soon, I hope.

> *Love,*
> *Louise*

A few days later, Rosanne wrote:

Louise,

Hi! Thought I'd drop you a note to let you know what's up. Read your manuscript. Not exactly what I expected but enlightening. If you don't mind I'm still going to use part of it in my research paper.

Have a good day. I'll talk to you soon.

> *Take care,*
> *Rosanne*

A welcome note. Any communication was a treasure at this point. Her message was not what I had hoped for, but it was equally enlightening. She had pulled back and that was understandable.

A few days later she called and said, "I don't hate you!"

She didn't say, "I love you."

She didn't say, "I understand."

She didn't say, "I've resolved my anger."

She said, "I don't hate you."

That was a start, and yet I wondered what she had done with the anger and hurt that stood before her the instant she consciously absorbed the abortion attempts and stopped reading the manuscript.

To this day, we have never delved into that labyrinth. It is hers, although I will gladly walk through it with her should she ever need me.

I later learned from Rose that she and Rosanne felt comfortable with the use of real names, locations and personal detail. I dropped my pseudonym and their loving permission allowed me to continue my manuscript in the light of total truth with the exception of changing the names and identifying facts of a few individuals in order to insure their privacy.

Though I have asked Rosanne if I could read her research paper on numerous occasions, I have never seen it. An inner wisdom tells me there is a divine right order to life, and I will receive it if I am meant to.

When I was very near completion of this book, I called my daughter and promised her a prepublication edition of the manuscript, which I knew she wanted. At the time I was still clarifying and rewriting the text, but was very near the end.

I looked forward to a short, casual call, but an inner wisdom, born of a newly-hatched strength, inspired questions I had only dreamed of touching. After the customary civilities, I began talking about the book and asked her to help me untangle some key points.

"What do you want to know?" she asked.

"What have you done with your anger about being adopted?" As soon as I phrased the question, I wished I had been more subtle.

"I've never been angry about being adopted. I've never felt adopted," she replied casually.

"What about that time when you were eighteen and your mother revealed my identify and you ran out of the kitchen saying, 'I never want to meet that woman, she threw me away.' That sounds angry to me." Again I was miles from being covert and amazed that I was actually having this conversation with Rosanne.

"I wasn't angry. I was just surprised." Her voice had a loud, persuasive tone.

"Then why did you rush out of the kitchen and not look at the folder and pictures? Weren't you a bit curious?" I knew I was pushing but could not resist this final question.

"I've always known I was adopted. I've always felt special and loved, and I've never been curious. I would never have looked for you. If it were not for my mother, I doubt that you or your family would be in my life at all."

Any questions I might have had concerning her feelings about the abortion attempts vaporized that instant. I had pushed as far as I wanted to. This was the end of that road, for now and perhaps forever.

Was I attempting to unearth feelings best left concealed? Was my daughter's anger nonexistent? Was I fabricating it? Were my assumptions inventions of the mind?

Only one thought surfaced—*give it up*. How Rosanne orchestrates this facet of her life is not mine to tamper with.

14

Merging and Harmonizing

Here is a test to find whether your mission on earth is finished: If you're still alive, it isn't.
—RICHARD BACH

All I know of love is that love is all there is.
—EMILY DICKINSON

Looking back, I can see that for a long period of time my life was much like a heart in need of resuscitation. Today, problems no longer evoke a sense of victimization in me. Instead, they present me with endless possibilities engineered to strengthen my core. Life's kaleidoscope of events has forced me to integrate that part centered around Rosanne with all the other parts.

It seems nothing ever stays the same or is ever definitely resolved. For me, guilt and regret have metamorphosed into an obligation to share the birth of an intriguing relationship. Whether Rosanne is angry or not—whether her anger is buried in the marrow of her soul—is immaterial. I love her just the way she is, and I am blessed that she is in my life. We are carving a path that few have walked before.

This past year has led to another birthday with Rosanne. There have been more notes and cards with the word "love" written once again. Rose has most recently told me that when she dies she is leaving her daughter to me. My only game plan for death is that both Rose and I go before Rosanne. That is as it should be, as seen from my human perspective. But having Rose lovingly trust me and her daughter's birthfamily is frosting on the cake. There seem to be no limitations to our relationship at this time.

That Rosanne is evolving into a heightened consciousness regarding her status as an adoptee became apparent one evening when Rose phoned. She shared an interesting communication which occurred after an emotionally charged television show had just aired.

"Rosanne and I watched "Baby M" together last night. She was quite interested in knowing how you would have decided that case."

I was intrigued by Rosanne's curiosity. I had also been drawn to the program. I took a deep breath and wondered if my opinion would affect Rosanne's impression of me. Then I switched gears and realized that it merited sharing since Rosanne was obviously inquisitive about my viewpoint.

"I would have given the baby to its mother with visitation rights for the father," I declared. "I'll tell Rosanne if you feel there is some value in sharing my point of view."

"I'm sure she'd like to hear from you." Rose was as open and loving as ever.

Because writing, for me, lends itself more easily to clarity than spoken words do, I comfortably communicated my feelings in a letter and mailed it the next day.

> *Dear Rosanne,*
>
> *I talked to your mother yesterday, and she expressed your interest on my assessment of the "Baby M" story. My opinion is legally irrelevant, but I'm pleased to share it with you.*
>
> *I feel the mother should be legally permitted to change her mind and keep her baby, with the child going to the father on weekends. The worst that could happen is that the child would have two families.*
>
> *I have a divorced friend with two young children (eight and ten), and the parents live within three blocks of one another. The children stay one week with their father and the other with their*

mother. They attend the same school, no matter where they live. The children are very flexible and have adapted happily.

Baby M's mother was portrayed as unstable, but I feel she has the potential to be loving. She was probably somewhat crazy from all the legal stress.

Personally, I can't imagine purposely having a child knowing I would give it away. The indelible regret of having surrendered you to adoption took me close to thirty years to heal.

My experience enables me to empathize with this woman. The surrender of you was predicated on the social and cultural mores of the sixties. Baby M's surrender is based on the binding legal document the mother had signed.

I cannot begin to judge the emotional aspects of a sticky legal issue. Life includes ample stress, and I feel anyone seeking or creating additional pressure merits close scrutiny.

Hope you are well.

Love,

Louise

I hoped my letter shed some light, especially regarding the complex issue of guilt. It matters to me that Rosanne understands I am no longer crippled with the culpability that haunted me for so long. Guilt may well be my Achilles' heel, for it seems to be forever testing me to this day. But, now, it is softened with self-love and that tames the dragon it once was.

I still cry occasionally but the tears are not born of guilt. I weep over the loss of my only child and that grief is self-loving. I am finally learning true compassion for myself. The tears are no longer tainted. They are cleansing.

15

From Memory into the Present

There is no end. There is no beginning. There is only the infinite passion of life.
—FEDERICO FELLINI

I dread success. To have succeeded is to have finished one's business on earth…
I like the state of continual becoming, with a goal in front, not behind.
—GEORGE BERNARD SHAW

There is a picture of Rosanne and me on my desk at school. My students have often looked at it and asked, "Is this your sister?"

"No," I answer each time, "that's my daughter."

Even now, ten years after our first meeting, I stare at the photo of us standing side by side. I am still awed. This is my daughter! The similarity proves it, somehow. Yet I am not her mother. That place belongs to Rose. I have reunited with a young woman who looks like me, who has many similar emotional characteristics and of whom I am more than fond. We have a spiritual and cellular bond.

When listening to myself on my telephone answering machine, I am struck with the similarity in our voices.

The magic of knowing my daughter has never diminished. The bridge that joins me to her and to Rose begins to show signs of use, as a formerly lost daughter merges with her birthfamily. I know now that adoption is a lifelong process, just as all aspects of our lives are continuous.

My journey has led me not so much out of my maze as into the true miracle of love—that most perfect magnet.

Recently Rosanne's love was transformed into vulnerability when she shared, "You've changed a lot since I first met you."

"You have, too," I said, smiling as we sat in her living room this past Christmas.

We had been talking about the term "lost lamb," the title of a previous version of my manuscript. That tenacious image eventually changed but on that afternoon it felt solid.

"I hate the concept of 'lost lamb,'" she said, not wanting to hurt my feelings but brave enough for honesty. "I've never felt lost."

"I know. You've never been lost. You were lost from my perspective."

I looked at her. She did not answer, but her face expressed understanding. Her next comment surprised me, but her integrity was unmistakable.

"I often feel that the gifts your parents give me are given from guilt."

I swallowed and looked at a young woman who was such a part of me and yet still resistant to her biological link. I know that my parents genuinely love Rosanne, and yet I had to search for words to communicate that clearly.

"My dad is terminally generous. Both of my parents have felt some guilt and regret, and yet their love and gifts are not predicated on anything negative. You're going to have to accept that you deserve their love, attention and gifts."

Rosanne was in a mood I had never seen before. She smiled at me and asked another question that I can only assume had long been on her mind.

"What would you have done if you had met me and found me to be a stringy-haired, illiterate slob?"

I knew that each verbalized fear could only clear a path that linked us together, not so much as daughter and birthmother, but as friends who trusted each other with the truth. Her question pleased me. It was the best one yet, and the only answer in my heart was another question for her.

"What if you had found me to be equally stupid and ugly? Would you not have wanted to know me and call me friend?"

She did not answer. But her smile warmed the room.

"Before I found you," I said, "I had only fantasy and visions of extremes. Yet, I knew that whatever I was to find, whoever I was to meet, would be perfect. Truth is always more palatable than daydreams."

Again, she did not answer, but her warmth spread through me.

These pages have chronicled the truth as I know it, and yet as I close this chapter in my life, I grapple with the concept of privacy. My most common fantasy is to live on a deserted island and have groceries air-lifted in once a month. But here I sit, writing my most private thoughts. Though employed as a school teacher, I have dared to write about abortion attempts and my less-than-perfect childhood. Clearly there has been a metamorphosis that has led me to the point where I allow my privacy to be touched. This brave move is my newest beginning, along with my hope for continued blossoming of my friendship with my daughter and my daughter's mother.

Once timid and awkward, trembling in a dark maze of my own making, I have been cultivated into a beautiful surprise mutation by the experiences of life. Truly, this is an astonishing endowment, and one that has enabled me to salute the miraculous seeds that can sprout in the most unlikely places.

This year I wrote to the Ross family. The last time I had been in their home was thirty years ago, when Mrs. Ross recognized my pain as labor and my mother rushed over to drive me to the hospital. My letter included a brief introduction as well as a synopsis of my reunion with Rose and Rosanne and a photograph of the three of us. A few weeks later I received a card signed Brian and Margaret. I did not recognize the names and was surprised to find that the card was indeed addressed to me. The content soon revealed the two strangers as Mr. and Mrs. Ross. Interestingly, they were unaware that I never knew their first names.

During all the months I stayed in their home, my immobilizing shyness and archaic sense of politeness hid their first names from me, and their agreement with the agency concealed my last name from them. I had never touched the mail or dared to look at such private matters. What a comical team we were!

But why, after so many years, did I have an impulsive urge to communicate with the Ross's? Cloaked in this exchange was another message provided by the universe. This one spanned a lifetime with my mother. Once again, life substantiated that there are no accidents.

Mrs. Ross' letter included a section that jumped out at me:

I remember, so well, the day your daughter was born. Your mother came back to tell me, and we both shed tears over a cup of tea.

Although I thought I knew my mother's pain, the depth of her sadness and the extent of her helplessness had never surfaced.

Obviously, my mother has never shared this with me. There are no quick answers to unraveling another person's motivations. But as I held the card, a deep mourning emerged from reading about her clandestine visit so long ago.

Why has she never spoken of this or any subject of consequence with me? Are we forever to wear blinders disclosing only safe issues of no real merit? What misfiring of love is this?

My mother is lost perhaps as much as Rosanne ever was, although she is lost on a level much more difficult to penetrate.

Why is truth so threatening? It is, I have learned, the pathway to love. It is the catalyst that created Rosanne's surprise call on Mother's Day last year.

Love itself is the miracle. It is the seed of transformation which directs each of us through the darkness towards the path that leads to our hearts. It is we who create the miracles—and it is love that makes these miracles possible.

Living at the Heart of Creation
by Michael Exeter

Living at the Heart of Creation is not a self-help manual or a "fix-it" book of superficial answers. It is, rather, an intelligent yet simple offering of insight into such challenging areas as the environmental crises, overpopulation, business relationships, and personal well-being. Michael Exeter shows exactly what it means to live at the heart of creation—to live at the place T. S. Eliot called "the still point of the turning world."

This book will be a friend and companion to anyone with the desire to explore what it means to be vibrant and wise in these extraordinary times.

$9.95

Gentle Roads to Survival
by Andre Auw, Ph.D.

Psychologist Andre Auw, a close associate of great 20th-century psychologists Carl Rogers and Virginia Satir, characterizes people who learn to prevail over life's challenges as survivors. While some are born survivors, for most of us, survival is a skill that must be learned. Using dozens of case histories, poems, and allegories, Auw identifies the lessons all survivors know: characteristics that distinguish people who give up hope from those who find the inspiration and encouragement to carry on.

"I loved your ideas. They contain a great deal of wisdom, wisdom gained from experience."   *—Carl Rogers*

$9.95

Your Body Believes Every Word You Say
by Barbara Levine

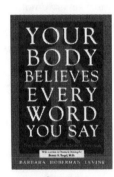

This is the first book to describe the language of the link between the mind and body. Barbara Levine's fifteen-year battle with a huge brain tumor led her to trace common phrases like "that breaks my heart" and "it's a pain in the butt" back to the underlying beliefs on which they were based and the symptoms they cause. She lists hundreds of common examples of words we use unconsciously every day, and shows how these "seedthoughts" can set us up for illness.

$11.95

Personal Power Cards
by Barbara Gress

A simple, easy to use set of flash cards for emotional wellness. Includes 55 cards, a carrying pouch, and an 80 page booklet. The Cards help retrain your feelings to be positive and healthy. Their combination of colors, shapes, and words allow positive thoughts to penetrate deep into your subconscious, "programming" your emotions for health.

"In the twenty years I have been using color and mind imagery with patients, I have never seen any approach have such a great benefit on self-discipline and self-esteem."
—Richard Shames, M.D.
Family Practitioner and author of Healing with Mind Power

$18.95

Voices From the Womb
by Michael Gabriel with Marie Gabriel
This is the first book to use extensive hypnotic regression to reveal the actual experiences of infants while in the womb. It shows that unborn infants are far more conscious and aware than has previously been recognized.

Michael Gabriel's exciting, unprecedented work traces the experiences of infants from the moment of conception through birth. It shows how deeply affected they are by their parents and the emotional harmony or confusion of adults.

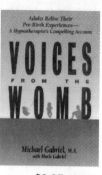

$9.95

Magnificent Addiction
by Philip R. Kavanaugh, M.D.
This book will decisively change the way you see addictions—forever. From the unique vantage point of a physician who has treated thousands of patients with emotional disorders, yet has undergone a major life-breakdown and healing himself, this revolutionary book takes all the assumptions that our society has about diagnosis and treatment and turns them upside down.

Speaking not as a detached clinical observer but as one who has gone through the painful and difficult experiences that life can bring, Dr. Kavanaugh forcefully argues for passionate addiction to life itself. The pages of this book sing with the power and purpose of a new and exciting message: that our most severe emotional crises are the very agents that stimulate us to reach for our highest good.

$12.95

Winds Across the Sky
by Chris Foster
Every so often a novel comes along that is simple, magical, utterly unique and compelling. *Winds Across the Sky* is that kind of rare, exceptional work. Woven around the themes of ecology, recovery, male-female relationships, and other great issues of the day, Chris Foster's lean prose and poetic style make this a book that pierces the heart of the reader.

This book portrays the fundamental unity of all creation in a new way and across a broader spectrum. It portrays loving communication as it occurs easily between different species and between humans and the natural world. Through tragedy and defeat, it potently affirms life's goodness and the inherent oneness of all creation.

$12.95 Hardback

Magic at our Hand
by Nancy Rose Exeter
Nancy Exeter, in a book which is as much a work of art as a work of prose, here expertly touches the essence of the universal feminine. With a gentle, clear voice, she calls every person to an awareness of the exquisite beauty to be found in every moment if we can only be aware. This book will inspire you, and prompt you to look on the world around you with the eyes of a child.

$11.95

More Than Just Sex
by Daniel Beaver, M.S., MFCC

The sexual revolution, says relationships counselor Daniel Beaver, has failed. While our generation is freer than ever before to explore and experiment with sex, our superficial liberation masks a chronic sense of failure and anxiety about unfulfilling sexual experiences.

With over eighteen years of experience in counseling a wide variety of relationship problems, the author brings together a depth and breadth of authoritative information not previously available from a single source about problems that most vex couples.

$12.95

Intuition Workout
by Nancy Rosanoff

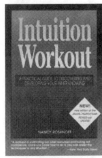

This book is a practical training manual. Its goal is to develop your intuition into a reliable tool that can be called upon at any time. It teaches people to automatically incorporate intuition into their decision-making process, as a source of awareness about what they feel at the deepest levels of personality. The core of the book is a series of simple exercises, which train and develop intuition to become strong and dependable. The author has been taking the mystery out of intuition in her workshops for executives, housewives, artists and others for more than ten years.

Book $10.95
90-min. Audiotape $9.95

Finding the Great Creative You
by Lynne Garnett, Ph.D.

Learn to live your passion! *Finding the Great Creative You* is a job and career book for the next phase of the economy. It is focused not on "getting a job" or "climbing the corporate ladder," but doing what you love most as a career path. Practical and down to earth, this outstanding book contains dozens of worksheets, exercises and visualizations that allow you to find your deepest purposes—and then actualize them in work. Thousands of people have had their lives changed by this book.

$10.95

Communing With the Spirit of Your Unborn Child
by Dawson Church

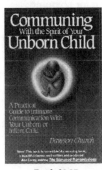

One of the most exciting works on pregnancy ever published, *Communing With the Spirit of Your Unborn Child* presents an inspiring vision of the spiritual magic of pregnancy, together with an extensive collection of exercises designed to facilitate communication between adults and children in the womb. It reveals the transcendental secrets behind child-rearing in a series of gentle, sensitive dialogues between a father and his son in the womb. Specific and concrete, it shows how to exchange and verify the information received. The accompanying audiotape contains some of the most deeply moving meditations ever recorded.

Book $8.95
90-min. Audiotape $9.95
Book & Tape set $15.95

Order Form

(Please print legibly)   Date _____

Name _____   Please send a catalog to my friend

Address _____   Name _____

City, St., Zip _____   Address _____

Phone _____   City, St., Zip _____

Quantity Discounts!

$2 off if you order 2 items
$3 off if you order 3 items
$4 off if you order 4 items, etc...

Item	Qty.	Price	Amount
Communing With the Spirit of Your Unborn Child (book)		$8.95	
Communing/Spirit Unborn Child (tape)		$9.95	
Communing/Spirit Unborn Child (book/tape set)		$15.95	
Finding the Great Creative You		$10.95	
Gentle Roads to Survival		$9.95	
Intuition Workout (book)		$10.95	
Intuition Workout (tape)		$9.95	
Living at the Heart of Creation		$9.95	
More Than Just Sex		$12.95	
Your Body Believes Every Word You Say		$11.95	
Personal Power Cards		$18.95	
Voices From the Womb		$9.95	
Magnificent Addiction		$12.95	
Winds Across the Sky		$12.95	
Magic at Our Hand		$11.95	

Add for shipping:
Book Rate: $2.50 for first item, $1.00 for ea. add. item.
First Class/UPS: $4.00 for first item, $1.50 ea. add. item.
Canada/Mexico: One-and-a-half times shipping rates.
Overseas: Double shipping rates.

Check type of payment:

☐ Check or money order enclosed

☐ Visa ☐ MasterCard

Acct. # _____

Exp. Date _____

Signature _____

Subtotal	
Quantity Discount	
Calif. res. add 7.25% sales tax	
Shipping	
Grand Total	

Send order to:
Aslan Publishing
PO Box 108
Lower Lake, CA 95457
or call to order:
(800) 275-2606

TFH